MAKING EQUALITY COUNT

MAKING EQUALITY COUNT

Irish and International Research
Measuring Equality and Discrimination

Edited by
Laurence Bond,
Frances McGinnity
and Helen Russell

The Liffey Press

Published by
The Liffey Press
Ashbrook House, 10 Main Street
Raheny, Dublin 5, Ireland
www.theliffeypress.com

A catalogue record of this book is
available from the British Library.

ISBN 978-1-905785-89-6

Printed in Ireland by Colour Books.

Contents

Acknowledgements

This book is based on the papers presented at a conference in Dublin in June 2010, entitled *'Making Equality Count'*. The aim of the conference was to examine international experience in measuring equality and discrimination and to highlight good practice developed in Ireland to date. The conference grew out of a joint research programme on equality and discrimination carried out by the Economic and Social Research Institute (ESRI) and the Equality Authority.

The conference itself was jointly organised by the Equality Authority, the ESRI, the Central Statistics Office (CSO) and the Geary Institute, University College Dublin (UCD) and was co-funded under the European Union Programme for Employment and Social Solidarity – PROGRESS (2007-2013). We graciously acknowledge this EU PROGRESS funding for both the conference and also for the production of this book.

We are very grateful to Eithne Tiernan and Tom McMahon of the CSO and Professor Colm Harmon of the UCD Geary Institute who worked with us in planning the conference. We would also like to thank the staff of the Equality Authority who assisted with organising and running the event.

Particular thanks are due to Ms Mary White TD, Minister for Equality, Integration and Human Rights, for agreeing to launch the conference. The conference sessions also benefited from a number of excellent chairs, to whom we are very grateful: Siobhan Carey, Assistant Director General of the CSO; Brian

Nolan, Professor of Public Policy at UCD; Professor Frances Ruane, Director of the ESRI; and Renée Dempsey, CEO of the Equality Authority.

Finally, we would like to most warmly thank our speakers and their co-authors – too numerous to mention here – for their first-rate conference presentations and for the expert and insightful contributions they have prepared for this publication.

This publication is supported under the European Union Programme for Employment and Social Solidarity – PROGRESS (2007– 2013). This programme is managed by the Directorate-General for Employment, Social Affairs and Equal Opportunities of the European Commission. It was established to financially support the implementation of the objectives of the European Union in the employment and social affairs area, as set out in the Social Agenda, and thereby contribute to the achievement of the Lisbon Strategy goals in these fields.

The seven-year Programme targets all stake holders who can help shape the development of appropriate and effective employment and social legislation and policies, across the EU-27, EFTA-EEA and EU candidate and pre-candidate countries.

PROGRESS mission is to strengthen the EU contribution in support of Member States' commitments. PROGRESS will be instrumental in:
– providing analysis and policy advice on PROGRESS policy areas;
– monitoring and reporting on the implementation of EU legislation and policies in PROGRESS policy areas;
– promoting policy transfer, learning and support among Member States on EU objectives and priorities; and
– relaying the views of the stakeholders and society at large.
For more information see:
http://ec.europa.eu/social/main.jsp?langId=en&catId=327
The information contained in this publication does not necessarily reflect the position or opinion of the European Commission.

About the Contributors

Dr. Ananthi Al Ramia is a Leverhulme Post-doctoral Research Associate at the Department of Experimental Psychology, University of Oxford. Ananthi's research interests lie broadly in the area of intergroup conflict and cooperation. Her research aims to uncover the role that ethno-religious diversity plays in explaining perceptions of intergroup trust and threat, and the extent to which these relationships are moderated by intergroup contact.

Laurence Bond has been Head of Research at the Equality Authority since 2002. Prior to this he worked for many years in research and policy analysis in the Irish public and non-government sectors.

Professor William Darity is Arts & Sciences Professor of Public Policy Studies and Professor of African and African American Studies and Economics at Duke University. His research focuses on inequality by race, class and ethnicity, stratification economics, schooling and the racial achievement gap, North-South theories of trade and development, skin shade and labour market outcomes, the economics of reparations, the Atlantic slave trade and the Industrial Revolution, doctrinal history and the social psychological effects of unemployment exposure.

Professor John F. Dovidio is currently Professor of Psychology at Yale University. Before that he was a professor at the University of Connecticut and at Colgate University where he also was

Provost and Dean of the Faculty. His research interests are in stereotyping, prejudice and discrimination; social power and nonverbal communication; and altruism and helping.

Dr. Brenda Gannon is a health economist, employed as Senior Project Leader at i3 Innovus, Stockholm since January 2010. She was previously Deputy Director at the Irish Centre for Social Gerontology, NUI Galway, where she was a leader in multidisciplinary and innovative research, and involved in strategic development, since 2006. Previous positions were at the Economic and Social Research Institute, Dublin (2000-2006), policy analyst at Forfas (1999-2000) and researcher at the Department of Economics, University of Newcastle-Upon-Tyne (1996-1998).

Professor Mary Gregory is Emeritus Fellow and Tutor in Economics at St Hilda's College in Oxford University. She has published extensively on employment and earnings, most recently particularly on women and part-time work. She is a founder-member of the European Low Wage Employment Network (LoWER).

Professor Miles Hewstone is Professor of Social Psychology and Fellow of New College in the University of Oxford. He has published widely in the general field of experimental social psychology. His major topics of research, thus far, have been attribution theory, social cognition, social influence, stereotyping and intergroup relations, and intergroup conflict.

Dr. Rebecca Chiyoko King-O'Riain is a Senior Lecturer in the Department of Sociology at the National University of Ireland, Maynooth. She has published on issues of race, racial categorization, mixed race, beauty pageants, Japanese Americans and immigrants in Ireland. Her book *Pure Beauty: Judging Race in Japanese American Beauty Pageants* (University of Minnesota Press) was published in 2006.

Dr. Frances McGinnity is Senior Research Officer and joint programme coordinator of Equality Research at the Economic and Social Research Institute, Dublin. Her research to date has examined labour market inequality, unemployment, temporary employment, part-time work, gender and racial discrimination, often from a comparative perspective. She is also interested in work-life balance, time-use and migrant integration.

Jacqueline Nelson was a Research Assistant at the ESRI when the experiment reported here was undertaken. She is now a doctoral student at the University of Western Sydney, and her doctoral work looks at anti-racism practice and policy in Australia. She has a Masters of Applied Social Research from Trinity College and an undergraduate degree in psychology from the University of Sydney.

Professor Brian Nolan is Professor of Public Policy in the School of Applied Social Science, University College Dublin. His research interests include poverty, income inequality, the economics of social policy, the Welfare State, health economics and health inequalities, disability, social indicators, and the EU's Social Inclusion Process.

Professor Louis A. Penner is Professor Family Medicine and Public Health Sciences at Wayne State University. He is also a Research Associate in the Research Centre for Group Dynamics at the Institute for Social Research, University of Michigan. His major research interests are prosocial behaviour and health disparities. He is the author or co-author of over 100 articles and chapters and eight books on these and related topics.

Emma Quinn is a Research Analyst at the Economic and Social Research Institute and National Coordinator of the Irish National Contact Point of the European Migration Network. Much of her research to date has examined migration and the Irish labour market, inequality and racial discrimination. She is also interested in integration-related issues.

Dr. Judith Rich is currently a Reader in the Department of Economics, University of Portsmouth. Her research interests are experimental economics, particularly field and natural experiments; discrimination in markets; efficiency wage theory and occupational sex segregation. She has published in all these areas.

Dr. Helen Russell is Associate Research Professor and joint programme coordinator of Equality Research at the Economic and Social Research Institute, Dublin. Her research covers a range of inter-connecting issues relating to equality, the labour market, the family and poverty/social inclusion. She has researched these topics in Ireland and in a comparative European context.

Dr. Dorothy Watson is Associate Research Professor at the Economic and Social Research Institute, Dublin. Her areas of interest are social inequality, values and belief systems, quality of life and survey methodology. Her current research projects include work on the measurement of income poverty in an international context, subjective well-being in Europe, workplace organisation/participation and gender and mental health in Ireland.

Chapter 1

Introduction: Making Equality Count

Laurence Bond, Frances McGinnity and Helen Russell

In spite of legislation outlawing discrimination across the EU, inequalities between groups appear to be an enduring feature of Irish and European societies. To what extent inequality is due to discrimination is a matter of continuing debate and controversy. Accurately measuring discrimination is therefore a crucial task, that is nonetheless very challenging. This has been a central task of a research programme on equality and discrimination carried out by the Economic and Social Research Institute and the Equality Authority, and was the theme of the conference 'Making Equality Count' held in Dublin in June 2010.

The conference presented findings from the Irish research programme and on international studies on equality and discrimination. The conference papers published in this volume, and the larger studies from which they are drawn, showcase exciting new research on inequality, and on discrimination as a contributor to that inequality. The chapters highlight the advances that have been made in the measurement of discrimination, as well as the depth of evidence that has been accumulated on this topic in recent decades. Together the chapters provide a nuanced and multi-dimensional picture of this complex process.

This introduction sets the scene for the chapters that follow. It reviews the legislative and policy context of equality in Ireland and Europe, It discusses a variety of methods used to measure inequality and discrimination, and the challenge of collecting appropriate data, before considering the themes of individual chapters.

Equality and Discrimination: The Changing Legislative Context

Prior to the 1970s, unequal treatment on the basis of gender and family status was enshrined in Irish legislation and policy. For example, the marriage bar which until 1973 required women to leave employment on marriage in certain sectors of the economy. Gender inequalities in pay were sanctioned by trade unions and employers in wage agreements. Accession to the EEC in 1973 was one of the key factors prompting legislative change in equality legislation in Ireland.

The Treaty of Rome required member states to provide for equal pay between men and women and in 1975 the Council adopted a directive on equal pay.[1] In the following year a directive on equal treatment in other aspects of employment was adopted which required that there should be no discrimination on the grounds of sex, either directly or indirectly by reference to marital or family status.[2] In Ireland, the 1972 White Paper on accession acknowledged that membership required the implementation of equal pay legislation, which had already been recommended by the Commission on the Status of Women (Mangan, 1993). The Anti Discrimination (Equal Pay) Act was passed in 1974 and this was followed by the 1977 Employment Equality Act, which implemented the Equal Treatment Directive. In later

---

[1] Council Directive 75/117/EEC of 10 February 1975.

[2] Council Directive 76/207/EEC of 9 February 1976.

years the legislative framework for gender equality has been enhanced through further Council directives – and consequent Irish legislation – on specific issues including social security matters, self-employment, pregnant workers, working time, parental leave, and part-time workers (McCrudden, 2003).

Internationally, demands for women's equality emerged alongside the broad post-war movement to combat racial and ethnic discrimination. Subsequently, the demand for equality and legal protection from discrimination was taken up by many other groups, including the lesbian and gay movement, people with disabilities and older people. The need for wider equality legislation was pressed in Irish public debate throughout the 1980s. This first bore fruit in 1989 when the Oireachtas passed an Act[3] outlawing incitement to hatred against a group of people on account of 'their race, colour, nationality, religion, ethnic or national origins, membership of the travelling community or sexual orientation'. Then in 1993 the Programme for Government agreed by Fianna Fail and the Labour Party included a commitment to introduce legislation to prohibit discrimination on a wide range of grounds. This legislation was finally enacted as the Employment Equality Act 1998 and the Equal Status Act 2000 (Crowley, 2006; Equality Authority, 2006).

Ireland's equality legislation prohibits discrimination on nine grounds: gender, marital status, family status, age, disability, sexual orientation, race, religion and membership of the Irish Traveller community. The Employment Equality Acts 1998-2008 cover all aspects of the employment relationship including advertising, access to employment, terms and conditions, equal pay, promotion, dismissal, training or work experience. The Equal Status Acts 2000-2008 prohibit discrimination in the provision of goods and services, accommodation and education.

---

[3] Incitement to Hatred Act (1989)

Initially, the EU did not have competence to legislate against discrimination on grounds not related to equality between men and women. This changed with the adoption of the Amsterdam Treaty, specifically Article 13, which stated that the Council acting unanimously 'may take appropriate action to combat discrimination based on sex, racial or ethnic origin, religion or belief, disability, age or sexual origin'. In 2000, the EU adopted two new Equality Directives which prohibit discrimination in employment on all of these grounds as well as discrimination in other aspects of daily life on the ground of racial or ethnic origin.[4] In 2002 an Amended Gender Equal Treatment Directive was adopted and a 2006 Directive recast existing European law on gender equality in employment.[5] A further new directive on equal treatment – prohibiting discrimination on grounds of age, disability, sexual orientation and religion or belief outside the employment sphere – is currently being negotiated.

From the outset – and still today – measurement issues have been central to debates on equal pay and labour market equality between men and women (Gregory, this volume; McGuinness et al., 2009). The extension of equality legislation to other grounds and to non-employment domains poses new measurement challenges. It is important to recognise that Irish and European equality legislation prohibits direct and indirect discrimination. Direct discrimination occurs where a person is treated less favourably than another person in a comparable situation on the basis of any of the discriminatory grounds. Indirect discrimination occurs where an apparently neutral provision puts a person under one of the nine grounds at a particular disadvantage com-

---

[4] Council Directive 2000/43/EC of 29 June 2000 (the 'Race Directive') and Council directive 2000/78/EC of 27 November 2000 (the 'Framework Employment Directive').

[5] Directive 2002/73/EC of 23 September 2002 and Directive 2006/54/EC of 5 July 2006.

pared with other persons, unless the provision is objectively justified by a legitimate aim and the means of achieving that aim are appropriate and necessary. From a measurement perspective, identifying indirect discrimination starts with the comparison of relevant outcomes across the grounds:

> In Europe, legal definitions of indirect discrimination assume, at least to some extent, that unequal outcomes, if persistently patterned along the lines of social traits, are prima facie evidence that the processes leading to those outcomes contain some kind of less favourable treatment of people with those traits (McLaughlin, 2007, p. 113).

Thus the first broad measurement challenge is to collect and analyse data on the economic and social position of the groups identified in equality legislation on a comparable basis. The second broad challenge is to develop robust measurement approaches and analytic techniques to capture the nature and extent of inequality and discrimination across the grounds. This indeed is the primary motivation for the collection of papers in this volume, and the conference from which they are drawn.

Measuring Equality and Discrimination

Inequality and discrimination can be investigated in a variety of different ways using a range of different methodologies each of which have different strengths and weaknesses, described briefly here.

In self-reports of discrimination, survey respondents are asked directly about their experience. This method has played an important role in tracking change (and stability) in the experience of discrimination over time. The analysis of self-reports can consider experiences of discrimination across the whole population and not just a specific minority group and can also investigate and compare self-reported discrimination across a variety of situations. However self-reports are subjective, depending on respondents' perception of their treatment by others. On the basis of assessment of objective indicators, some groups appear to under-report discrimination, while others appear to over-report. Good survey design can help minimise these weaknesses but they cannot be eliminated.

A second technique to investigate discrimination is through the statistical analysis of differential outcomes. This is probably the most common method used to measure discrimination in the social sciences (see Altonji and Blank, 1999; Quillan, 2006; Pager and Shepherd, 2008) The method compares measures of outcomes across groups and statistically adjusts for non-discriminatory sources of difference, e.g. education, skills, experience etc. Residual differences that remain after these factors are controlled are commonly attributed to discrimination. There have been important developments in this methodology over recent years, such as quantile regression techniques, propensity score matching and other selection correction techniques, as well as the development of new datasets (e.g. within-organisation data, longitudinal data on work careers and earnings). These advances significantly enhance estimates of the element of inequality that cannot be explained by individuals characteristics or previous selection processes. However, it remains difficult to prove conclusively that this residual is due to discrimination.

The third methodology commonly used to measure discrimination are surveys of the general population, or subgroups, e.g. employers (Young and Morrell, 2005) which investigate attitudes and beliefs about the 'out-group'. Surveys of this type can also investigate in-group biases in the form of more favourable attitudes towards the majority group. While these types of studies can be informative, they, like the other methods, have limitations. Such attitude reports are subject to 'social desirability' biases, whereby respondents are reluctant to express attitudes or opinions that are contrary to the prevailing ideology of equality Best practice in these surveys can reduce but not entirely eliminate such biases.

Furthermore, discriminatory behaviour cannot simply be deduced from attitudes although there is a significant correlation Therefore additional techniques have been developed to measure implicit attitudes or to bypass attitudes and measure discriminatory behaviour directly through field experiments.

Field studies can provide direct evidence on discrimination which is difficult to challenge. Instead of measuring attitudes, these studies measure the actual response of employers or service providers to carefully matched candidates who differ only in respect to the characteristic on which discrimination is thought to occur – gender, race, nationality, age etc. These experiments occur in real-life situations, for example applications are sent in response to actual job vacancies, and the responses are observed. These studies show consistent evidence of discrimination against the out-group in a wide variety of situations. While these methodologies can provide powerful evidence on discrimination, field studies can only be carried out within certain situations (e.g. applications for housing, job applications, accessing services/products, grading) at the initial point of contact, and cannot be used to detect discrimination in other processes, e.g. promotions. Furthermore, such studies focus on individual discriminatory decisions and cannot investigate the wider structural influences or psychological antecedents.

The psychological processes involved in discrimination have been investigated using a variety of laboratory techniques, including Implicit Association Tests. These test the time taken by respondents/subjects to make a link between different groups and stereotypical adjectives, and generally find that it takes subjects longer to associate the 'out-group' with a positive characteristic than with a negative characteristic.[6] However, there is

---

[6] The test subjects are generally from the dominant group. The results on the implicit attitudes of subordinate groups are more mixed, although there is some evidence of biases against the out-group even amongst its members.

continuing debate on the relationship between implicit prejudice (measured using such tests) and explicit attitudes, and the
extent to which they influence behaviour (Quillan, 2006, pp. 317-
19; Al Ramiah et al., this volume).

All the above methods are considered in later chapters.
Other methods not included in this volume which nevertheless
provide important insights into discrimination include analysis
of legal cases (e.g. Banks and Russell, forthcoming), and qualitative studies which investigate the nature of discrimination and
unequal treatment (for example, Davis et al., 2005; MRCI, 2004;
MacLachlan and O'Connell, 2000), or case-studies of employers
and organisations (e.g. Collinson et al., 1990; O'Connor, 1996).
These studies can provide very detailed evidence on subtle and
multi-dimensional processes involved in discrimination.

Each of these methods have strengths and weaknesses, which
mean building a comprehensive picture and deeper understanding of discrimination and inequality requires a triangulation of
results across different methods.

Equality Data Collection

While collection of age and gender data is now fairly standard in
official and related social statistics – whether survey-based or
drawn from administrative sources – this is far from the case in
regard to other grounds such as disability, race and ethnicity,
sexual orientation or religion (NSB, 2003). That said, over the
last decade the Central Statistics Office in Ireland (CSO) has
made real progress in the collection of equality data. The inclusion of equality variables is most advanced in the Census (see
CSO, 2007), which includes classificatory variables for all
grounds except sexual orientation,[7] although the collection of

---

[7] On sexual orientation, household relationship questions in the Census do currently allow for the identification of same- sex couples living together

equality date is less developed in the key social surveys.[8] Self-reported discrimination is a social indicator that is of particular relevance to equality. In 2004, the CSO included a module on equality within the Quarterly National Household Survey which provided the first nationally representative estimates of the experience of discrimination across a range of life domains (see Russell et al., this volume).

There are particular challenges in collecting representative data on minority groups that constitute a small proportion of the population or are hard-to-reach, for example members of the Traveller community or small religious minority groups. Household surveys of a general population are unlikely to pick up sufficient numbers of these groups. Cultural factors, fear of disclosure, health problems and language/literacy issues can also pose barriers to participation in surveys for certain individuals and groups. These barriers also lead to under-representation of some groups, particularly the most disadvantaged, from the surveys that form the basis of much of the research on inequalities in the public sphere in Ireland.

In some cases these non-response biases can be corrected through weighting. In other cases even the Census figures are believed to be under-reported[9] and there have been intense efforts to include hard-to-reach groups. For example, the All-

---

[8] The Quarterly National Household Survey (QNHS) includes questions on age, sex, marital status, nationality and family composition. Additional equality variables are periodically collected with the QNHS Social Modules. The survey of Income and Living Conditions (EU-SILC) collects data on gender, age, marital status, family status, nationality and on chronic illness. In the National Employment Survey (NES) Employees' age, gender and nationality is collected but not other equality variables.

[9] For example, nationality/ethnicity survey figures are routinely weighted back to the Census figures although rapid changes in migration meant that even these figures are likely to be increasingly inaccurate. While Kobayashi (2005) argues that the number of members of the Traveller community are underreported in the Census.

Ireland Study on Traveller Health trained 400 Traveller Peer Researchers to carry out a Census among members of the Travelling Community. Data on sexual orientation is rarely collected in Irish quantitative surveys and therefore a significant data gap remains on this issue and restricts the research that can be conducted on inequality and discrimination on this important ground.

The continued investment in collecting high quality survey and administrative data across the range of grounds covered by equality legislation is therefore a prerequisite for continued advances in research and to enhance policy-making to reduce inequality and discrimination.

Overview of the Chapters

This volume draws on Irish and international research on inequality that adopts a range of different methods to address the key questions about the incidence, distribution and effects of discrimination and inequality, as well as considering some of its antecedents. Overall, a range of grounds are included: particular papers focus on gender, disability and ethnicity/nationality; one paper focuses on the intersection between two grounds; still others consider a range of grounds. Some papers report single studies or projects; some present an overview of research in the area. Four papers focus on Ireland; others report research from the US, the UK or a range of other Western countries. What the papers share is an overall concern with measuring equality and discrimination. The first four papers focus on explicitly measuring and describing the extent of discrimination; the latter four focus primarily on equality, though reflect on discrimination.

In the first paper in the volume, Russell and her colleagues present self-reported discrimination in Ireland for a range of domains using high-quality survey data representing the whole population. While self-reports are subjective, and in essence reflect an individual's experience of discrimination, this survey followed best practice to minimise bias: questions were limited to specific domains and referred to a particular time period. Respondents were asked about their experience of discrimination in the workplace; in looking for work; in shops, pubs, restaurants; using financial services (banks etc); in relation to education; obtaining housing' accessing health services; using transport services; and accessing other public services.

The highest reported discrimination was in recruitment (5.8 per cent of those who had been seeking work); then discrimination in the workplace (5 per cent). In the services, the highest reported discrimination was in accessing accommodation (4 per cent) and financial services (3.7 per cent). The authors note that people with disabilities and non-Irish nationals experience discrimination in a wide variety of domains. For other groups, discrimination is more context-specific. Another salient finding is that only 40 per cent of those experiencing discrimination reported this to anyone and the social groups with the highest rates of discrimination are the least likely to take action.

Given the limitations of self-report data, the authors are careful to compare their findings to those from different sources in their conclusion. In general, the findings on self-reported discrimination are consistent with those from other studies of objective outcomes in Ireland – for gender, non-Irish nationals and people with disabilities. However, the comparison suggests that older people and those with low education are likely to under-report discrimination – an issue the authors reflect on in their conclusion. The results of the survey reported in this paper, and in the accompanying report (Russell et al., 2008), provide an important benchmark for examining changes in the nature of discrimination experience in the future. The survey is being repeated in late 2010.

The next two papers show how field experiments may overcome some of the difficulties with measuring discrimination by comparing outcomes. Judith Rich presents an interesting overview of the field experiment method, and what experiments in the last 50 years have to tell us about discriminatory behaviour in markets. In field experiments two individuals who are identical on all characteristics other than the potential for discrimination (race, ethnicity, sex, age, sexual orientation or disability) apply for the same job, housing or product. Responses are recorded and discrimination measured as the extent to which one individual is successful relative to the other. The tests can be conducted by personal approaches or by phone (audits), or by using written applications (correspondence tests). Matching the applicants carefully is crucial, whether the test is a personal or a written application.

Rich reports that results from the first wave of experiments (1966 to 2000) in a range of Western countries found that overwhelmingly for minorities and women, access to jobs was restricted, access to housing was restricted and they paid more for products. These findings are broadly consistent with the findings of research on differential outcomes, for example in employment. More recent studies, conducted between 2000 and 2010, found access to jobs was restricted for racial minorities, women, older and obese individuals; access to housing was restricted for racial minorities and homosexuals; and that racial minorities, women and older individuals pay more for products.

Rich concludes that it is alarming that the more recent tests report similar findings to earlier studies, given public concern about discrimination and legislative developments in the area. As it is often very difficult for an individual to know they have been discriminated against, particularly given concealment by employers, this raises the issue of whether measures to deal with discrimination in legislation and in practice are adequate.

In the first experiment of its kind in Ireland, McGinnity and her colleagues test for discrimination in recruitment against minority groups. Ireland is an interesting case, as the recent economic boom was accompanied by rapid immigration of a nationally diverse population into a country overwhelmingly White and Irish. The researchers sent out almost 500 equivalent CVs in response to advertised vacancies for jobs in administration, finance and retail sales in the greater Dublin area.

They find that candidates with Irish names are over twice as likely to be asked to attend an interview as are candidates with an African, Asian or German name. The discrimination rate is relatively high by international standards, and does not vary across occupation. Interestingly, they find no difference in the degree of discrimination between minority candidates, and argue that this may be linked to the recent nature of immigration in Ireland and the lack of established minority groups.

The paper by Al Ramiah and colleagues adds insights from social psychology to our understanding of discrimination. Their comprehensive overview covers definitions of discrimination, psychological theories, measurement issues and consequences of discrimination. Social psychologists are careful to distinguish prejudice (an attitude) from stereotype (a belief) and discrimination (a behaviour). Influential theories of discrimination include the social identity perspective (the drive for positive social identity can result in discrimination against the outgroup); the social justification perspective (groups adopt a social identity commensurate with their position in society); aversive racism (upholding egalitarian norms while maintaining subtle prejudice); and BIAS maps (the status and competitiveness of the group predicts stereotypes of warmth and competence, which influences affect and thus action).

The paper discusses ways in which these concepts have been operationalised/measured. Measures include explicit measures of prejudice, which are self-reports of attitudes constructed in a way to reduce socially desired responding. Implicit tests, like the Implicit Association Test, tap the possibly unconscious and unintentional parts of a person's prejudice. The authors' review of laboratory and field experiments reveals that explicit prejudice predicted verbal behaviour while implicit prejudice predicted non-verbal friendliness. In experiments on helping behaviour, the evidence supports the predictions of aversive racism theory.

Overall, the correlation between both explicit and implicit prejudice and discrimination is modest, and significantly not all individuals who hold negative attitudes go on to discriminate. What is clear though is that discrimination may have serious consequences in terms of mental and physical health, self-esteem and underperformance for the minority group, and the disadvantage experienced by any one group may translate into intergenerational disadvantage. Measuring the extent of discrimination, a key focus of this volume, is therefore an extremely valuable exercise.

In his paper on racial inequality, William Darity describes the widespread perception that the US is a 'post-racial' society, and illustrates this cogently for the general population using survey data. He argues that this perception also permeates much of conventional economics. It does so in two major ways. First, the individual is at the core of economic thinking. The individual is the decision maker, the focus of attention, the unit of analysis – not a racial or ethnic group, or a social class. Second, conventional economic theory argues that market competition drives out discriminatory practice: profits and prejudice are mutually exclusive.

Darity's 'stratification economics' research programme was developed in response to deficiencies identified in conventional economic approaches to discrimination. In stratification economics the centrality of the group as a source of identity belonging and resources is key. So also is the question of how group membership is determined, whether by self-classification or social classification. Streams of research in this programme use a range of methods and include investigating wealth inequality; examining differential outcomes in attainment in schooling and segregration patterns within and between schools; racial disparities in self-employment patterns; and the effect of skin shade on outcomes in labour and marriage markets. One set of studies compares self-reports of wage discrimination with independent estimates of discriminatory differences in wages. Evidence from this body of research strongly refutes the idea that the US has become a post-racial society. In conclusion, Darity argues that a post-racial society is not the ideal, and he calls instead for a 'race fair', not a 'race blind', society.

The final three papers in this volume present empirical evidence on differential outcomes across groups, focusing on gender inequality (Gregory), disability (Gannon and Nolan) and the intersection between gender and disability (Watson and Lunn). In her searching review of the gender pay gap, Gregory considers recent evidence, from the UK and other European countries, given methodological advances and new sources of data. Where is the pay gap greatest and what are the mechanisms underlying it? Recent research using quantile regression clearly shows that the pay gap is greatest at the upper end of the earnings distribution, supporting the idea of a 'glass ceiling' on women's earnings. A study using personnel records from a US grocery store finds that men are much more likely to be promoted than women, suggesting that part of the earnings gap is due to differential rates of promotion. Occupational downgrading, often associated with a shift to part-time work following childbirth, also plays an important role in understanding the gender pay penalty in the UK. An earnings gap remains even after return to full-time work with the occupational downgrading reversed.

The family pay penalty is an important component of the gender pay gap: research in Germany finds a significant wage drop following maternity leave; this diminishes with time back in work, although a penalty for work experience foregone remains. In Denmark, on the other hand, the only effect of children on mother's earnings is through lost work experience. Gregory concludes that in a social climate supportive of working mothers, as in the Scandinavian countries, the pay penalty to maternity leave can be minimal. In looking to the future, Gregory is optimistic, arguing that the 'quiet revolution' in the status of women is set to continue, given the rapid rise in educational qualifications of women and technological advances favouring women's employment

Gannon and Nolan summarise a number of research studies in Ireland concerned with how the experience of people with a long-term disability or illness differs from that of other people. The paper reviews evidence from a range of life domains: education, earnings, poverty and social participation. They draw a crucial distinction between those who had an illness or disability that limits everyday activities and those whose disability does not. Using econometric models, the authors found that, after accounting for age and gender, those with a chronic illness or disability that hampered everyday activities were much more likely to have low educational qualifications than those with no illness or disability. They are much less likely to be in employment and also more likely to be in poverty than those with no disability. Once the individuals have a job, the impact of disability on wages is less marked than for education and employment. Disability also limited social participation (club membership, contact with neighbours and friends/relatives, nights out, voting behaviour), particularly for those with a severely hampering illness or disability.

Using the panel element of the data, the authors demonstrate how not just the fact of being disabled but the *onset* of disability is associated with negative outcomes like employment loss. In their conclusion, the authors note that the nature of this disadvantage and the factors underlying it are complex. The role of discrimination as opposed to other factors is difficult to isolate. Designing policies to combat this disadvantage is also challenging, particularly in the current economic climate. Yet the experience in other countries has shown that, given adequate social investment and attitudinal changes, the disadvantage associated with disability can be greatly reduced.

In policy debates on discrimination and disadvantage, the notion of multiple disadvantage has gained considerable appeal, though is rarely tested empirically across a range of outcomes. In their paper using 2006 Irish Census data, Watson and Lunn operationalise some of these ideas. Does membership of two disadvantaged groups increase the risk of a negative outcome, and if so, is this increase in risk additive or exponential? They test this, examining differences by gender and disability status for four outcomes: risk of low education, labour market participation, unemployment and being in low skilled employment.

They find that the most common pattern was that of 'non-additive' disadvantage: membership in both groups is associated with less disadvantage than the sum of risks associated with membership in each separately. There were also examples of additive disadvantage, where membership in both groups is associated with a level of disadvantage approximately equal to the sum of the two risks. There was only one weak example of exponential disadvantage, where members of both groups are even more disadvantaged than one would expect from combining the effects of membership in each group. Watson and Lunn conclude that it is difficult to generalise about multiple disadvantage, as patterns of disadvantage vary substantially across outcomes. And while disadvantage may not be additive, any one group may experience high levels of disadvantage on one ground alone. Indeed, an interesting lesson from their paper is that the notion of multiple disadvantage may be simple but its application to real-life data is complex. Exploring multiple disadvantage can draw attention to the fact that the interaction of education, labour market and life-cycle processes may result in unexpected outcomes.

In summary, this book contributes to the literature on equality and discrimination in a number of ways. Firstly, it demonstrates the different approaches to measurement, and highlights their strengths and weaknesses. Secondly, it reviews a wide body of evidence on equality and discrimination. Thirdly, it demonstrates how important the collection of adequate data is for the whole project. Fourthly, it draws policy implications of the findings. Policy on equality and discrimination needs to be informed by convincing evidence, and innovative research can provide that evidence.

References

Altonji, G.J. and Blank, R.M. (1999) 'Race and Gender in the Labor Market', in O. Ashenfelter and D. Card (eds.) *Handbook of Labor Economics,* 3C, pp. 3143-3259.

Banks and Russell (forthcoming) *Pregnancy Related Discrimination in the Workplace: A Review of Legal Cases in Ireland 1998 to 2008,* Dublin: HSE Crisis Pregnancy Programme and The Equality Authority.

Collinson, D., Knights, D. and Collinson, M. (1990) *Managing to Discriminate,* London: Routledge.

Crowley, N. (2006) *An Ambition for Equality,* Dublin: Irish Academic Press.

Central Statistics Office (2007) *Equality in Ireland 2007,* Dublin: Stationery Office.

Davis, S., Neathey, F., Regan, J. and Willison, R. (2005) *Pregnancy Discrimination at Work: A Qualitative Study,* Manchester: Equal Opportunities Commission.

Equality Authority (2006) *Traveller Ethnicity: An Equality Authority Report,* Dublin: The Equality Authority.

Koybayashi, Y. (2006) *Demographic Advice for the Traveller's All-Ireland Health Study,* Discussion Paper, Dublin: Department of Health and Children.

McCrudden, C. (2003) 'Theorising European Equality Law', in C. Costello and E. Barry (eds.) *Equality in Diversity: The New Equality Directives,* pp. 1-38, Dublin: The Equality Authority and Irish Centre for European Law.

McGuinness, S., Kelly, E., Callan, T. and O'Connell, P.J. (2009) *The Gender Wage Gap in Ireland: Evidence from the National Employment Survey 2003,* Dublin: The Equality Authority and The Economic and Social Research Institute.

McLachlan, M. and O'Connell, M. (2000) *Cultivating Pluralism: Psychological, Social and Cultural Perspectives on a Changing Ireland*, Dublin: Oak Tree Press.

McLaughlin, E. (2007) 'From Negative to Positive Equality Duties: The Development and Constitutionalisation of Equality Provisions in the UK', *Social Policy and Society* 6:1, pp. 111-121.

Mangan, I. (1993) 'The influence of EC membership on Irish social policy and social services' in S. Ó'Cinnéide (ed.) *Social Europe: EC Social Policy and Ireland*, pp. 60-81, Dublin: Institute of European Affairs.

Migrant Rights Centre Ireland (2004) *Private Homes – A Public Concern*, Dublin: MRCI.

National Statistics Board (2003) *Developing Irish Social and Equality Statistics to Meet Policy Needs: Report of the Steering Group on Social and Equality Statistics*, Dublin: Stationery Office.

O'Connor, P. (1996) 'Organisational Culture as a Barrier to Women's Promotion' *Economic and Social Review*, Vol. 27, No. 3, pp. 187-216.

Pager, D. and Shepherd, H. (2008) 'The Sociology of Discrimination: Racial discrimination in Employment, Housing, Credit and Consumer Markets', *Annual Review of Sociology*, Vol. 34, pp. 181-209.

Quillan, L. (2006) 'New Approaches to Understanding Racial Prejudice and Discrimination', *Annual Review of Sociology*, Vol. 32, pp. 299-328.

Russell H., Quinn, E., King O'Riain, R. and McGinnity, F. (2008) *The Experience of Discrimination in Ireland: Analysis of the QNHS Equality Module*, Dublin: The Equality Authority and The Economic and Social Research Institute.

Young, V. and Morrell, J. (2005a) *Pregnancy Discrimination at Work: A Survey of Employers*, Working Paper Series No. 20, Manchester: Equal Opportunities Commission.

Chapter 2

The Experience of Discrimination in Ireland: Evidence from Self-Report Data

*Helen Russell, Frances McGinnity, Emma Quinn
and Rebecca King O'Riain*[1]

The mid-1990s to the mid-2000s was a period of significant development and increasing awareness of the problem of discrimination within Irish society. This is reflected in the development of equality legislation and the establishment of bodies such as the Equality Authority and the Equality Tribunal. Discrimination is commonly understood as differential treatment on the basis of group membership that unfairly disadvantages a group, and is defined in Irish law as covering unfair treatment in employment, training, accessing goods, services, accommodation and education across nine grounds: gender, marital status, family status, age, disability, race/ethnicity/nationality, sexual orientation, religious belief, and membership of the Traveller community (see Bond et al., this volume). However, while expectations of a fair society for all have become increasingly well-defined in recent years, relatively little is known of the nature or extent of the

[1] The authors would like to acknowledge the Equality Authority who funded the research as part of the Research Programme on Equality and Discrimination with the ESRI. We would also like to thank the CSO for access to the micro-data from the QNHS and to the European Foundation for access to the European Working Conditions Survey micro-data.

problem of discrimination in Ireland. This is partly because measuring discrimination offers considerable challenges to researchers, as discriminatory behaviour is rarely observed directly. A number of methods for measuring discrimination have been used in previous research, though no single approach allows researchers to address all the important measurement issues and each have their strengths and weaknesses (see Bond et al., this volume; Blank et al., 2004; Darity and Mason, 1998; Pager and Shepherd, 2008).

Surveys of respondents' self-reported experiences of discrimination are an important instrument in the toolkit for measuring inequality and discrimination in society. This chapter draws on data from the first nationally representative survey designed to collect information on self-reports of discrimination in Ireland, which was carried out by the Central Statistics Office (CSO) in 2004.

The method draws on the respondents' own experiences and their interpretation of events. The primary strengths of this methodology are its breadth and the representative nature of the results. Surveys of discrimination or unfair treatment can investigate a wide variety of situations and are not confined to a particular setting such as employment or housing. One survey can ask respondents about their experiences across a wide range of domains.

General population surveys also have the advantage of collecting information across all sectors of society and not just among an identifiable minority group. The results of surveys conducted upon a nationally representative random sample of the population can be generalised to the wider population, which is a key limitation of some other approaches to investigating discrimination such as experimental studies, legal caseload analyses and qualitative studies. A further advantage of this approach is that follow-up questions can be asked about respondents' reactions to discriminatory experiences and the perceived consequences for the individual.

The subjective nature of self-reports is the chief weakness of this methodology – unlike legal cases, there is no independent arbitrator to assess whether discrimination took place according to a set of defined criteria and evidence. Self-reports of discrimination may be subject to incomplete information and bias. Discrimination may be under-reported because it is not observable to the respondent (for example, an employer might discriminate against a job candidate who is female/pregnant/a non-national but the applicant will not know the reason he or she has not been hired). Others may experience discriminatory treatment but not identify this as discrimination due to lack of knowledge about rights or because they wrongly believe the treatment was due to some other factor. Alternatively, discrimination may be over-reported if, in an ambiguous situation, respondents falsely attribute their treatment to discrimination when it is in fact due to some other reason (for example, denial of job promotion could be due to poor performance rather than discrimination). Such under- or over-reporting is especially problematic if it varies systematically across the groups of interest. For example, previous research shows that the highly educated tend to report more discrimination in a range of situations, despite being objectively advantaged (McGinnity et al., 2006). A further disadvantage of this approach is that it is confined to discrimination that operates at an individual level. Discrimination that operates at a structural/institutional level (for example, occupational segregation) which disadvantages a group is unlikely to be reported in this type of survey.

The limitations of self-report and other single methods of investigating discrimination mean that it is important to interpret the results in conjunction with findings generated through other research methodologies, a process known as triangulation. In general, researchers have found direct self-reports of discrimination to be accurate and reliable when cross validated against other data sources (Blank et al., 2004).

Previous research has found widely varying levels of self-reported discrimination depending on country, the social situation investigated and the way in which the questions are asked. These type of surveys are most frequently fielded in the US, although a number of cross-European studies have also been conducted. The studies are often linked to specific types of discrimination, for example on the basis of gender or race/ethnicity (see Pager and Shepherd, 2008; Blank et al., 2004 for reviews; see also Darity, this volume).

For example, in a national population survey of adults in the US (N=3,032), Kessler et al. examine perceived discrimination across a range of eleven domains (e.g. promotion, job hire, denied bank loan, denied/received inferior medical care, other services) across the respondent's whole lifetime. The rate of reported discrimination was highest in respect of job hires (16 per cent), promotion (13 per cent) and other services (9 per cent), and fell to 3 per cent in the case of medical care. A European study on migrants' self-reports of racism and discrimination was conducted across 12 EU Member States including Ireland (EUMC, 2006). Altogether more than 11,000 respondents with migrant backgrounds answered questions about their experience of discrimination in the preceding year across five domains: employment, private life and public arenas, shops and restaurants, commercial transactions and institutions.[2] While the questions were harmonised, the selected migrant groups and the sampling methods differed across the countries. The Irish sample consisted of four migrant groups, North African, Asian, Central/South African and Eastern European, who had come to Ireland through either the work-permit system or the asylum process (see McGinnity et al., 2006 for further details). Among other results, the Irish report found that 35 per cent of migrants experi-

---

[2] Within these five categories respondents were questioned about 16 different experiences.

enced harassment on the street/on public transport/in public places in the past year; 32 per cent of those entitled to work experienced harassment at work, while 21 per cent of this group reported discrimination in access to employment; 15 per cent reported being denied access to housing because of their national/ethnic origin, and a similar percentage reported being denied credit/a loan, or being harassed by neighbours; 14 per cent reported being refused entry to a restaurant, pub, or nightclub during the last year because of their national/ethnic origin. Rates of self-reported discrimination were highest among Black Africans (ibid, p. vi).

In another European-wide study, which is repeated every five years, the European Working Conditions Survey 2005 found that 5 per cent of those in employment felt they had been discriminated against 'at work' in the previous 12 months across a range of grounds (religion, ethnic background, sexual orientation, disability, nationality, sex).[3] In Ireland, 6.8 per cent of employees reported discrimination at work, and rates ranged from 2.1 per cent in Spain to 9.1 per cent in the Czech Republic. The earlier surveys reveal that the rates of self-reported discrimination in Ireland increased over time, from 2.9 per cent in 1995 to 4.4 per cent in 2000 and 6.8 per cent in 2005.

Perceived discrimination has also been found to have negative outcomes. Kessler et al. (1999) report that self-reported discrimination is linked to depression, anxiety and other negative health effects. Perceived discrimination has also been linked to diminished effort in education or in the labour market, which can have a further negative impact on outcomes (Loury, 2002; Steele, 1997).

---

[3] Findings based on authors' own analysis of the European Working Conditions Survey micro-data supplied by the European Foundation for the Improvement of Living and Working Conditions (contact first author for further details). The results refer to the proportion of respondents who report discrimination at work on any of the grounds.

This chapter is primarily concerned with identifying the socio-demographic factors associated with greater risk of self-reported discrimination in Ireland. We are particularly interested in the extent to which groups identified in the equality legislation self-report that they have been discriminated against in the recent past. In discussing these results we examine whether they are consistent with other evidence on discrimination and inequality in Ireland using alternative methodologies. As the survey was the first of its kind in Ireland, the results are important for benchmarking future changes in discrimination experiences.

The Survey

The results are based on analysis of the CSO Quarterly National Household Survey, Equality Module, conducted in the fourth quarter of 2004. The QNHS is a nationally representative random sample of private households in Ireland. The Equality Module of the survey was completed by 24,600 respondents, all aged 18 years and over who were interviewed directly.

The survey follows international best practice to minimise bias in the estimates of discrimination:

- Respondents were provided with an explicit definition of discrimination and a number of concrete examples of what is and is not considered discrimination (see Table 1).

- The experience of discrimination is linked to specific social contexts or domains (Table 2).

- The questions are time-delimited – in this case, confined to the two years preceding the interview (Table 2).

Table 1: Definition of Discrimination on Equality Module (Prompt Card)

Discrimination takes place when one person or a group of persons are treated less favourably than others because of their gender, marital status, family status, age, disability, 'race' – skin colour or ethnic group, sexual orientation, religious belief, and/or membership of the Traveller community.

Discrimination can occur in situations such as where a person or persons is/are refused access to a service, to a job, or is/are treated less favourably at work. In other words, discrimination means treating people differently, negatively or adversely because they are for instance Asian, Muslim, over 50 years of age, a single parent, and/or homosexual.

If the reason you may have been treated less favourably than someone else is due to another reason (such as your qualifications, being over an income limit or because you are further back in a queue for something) this does not constitute discrimination.

Respondents were asked about the experience of discrimination across nine social situations or domains. Two of these were work-related and the remaining seven related to accessing services (see Table 2). For those who reported discrimination in any of these situations, follow up questions were asked concerning the grounds on which they felt they were discriminated, the effect the experience had, and their response. The respondents were not asked who was responsible for the discrimination, therefore it is possible, for example, that discrimination 'at work' was instigated by an employer/manager or by colleagues or customers, etc. Similarly, service discrimination may have been instigated by the service provider or by other users.

In addition to the specific questions on subjective experiences of discrimination, the module also included some classificatory information not routinely collected in the QNHS. This included two questions on disability, detailed information on religious affiliation and a question on ethnicity. The QNHS measure of 'ethnicity' is self-selected from a set of 11 pre-coded categories using the classification applied in the 2006 Irish Census (see Garner, 2004, for a discussion of the use of the term ethnicity in Ireland and Russell et al., 2008 for further details of the measure in the survey).

Table 2: Questions on Experience of Discrimination

In the past *two years*, have you personally felt discriminated against:

1. In the workplace?

2. While looking for work?

3. In places like, shops, pubs or restaurants?

4. Using services of banks, insurance companies or other financial institutions?

5. In relation to education?

6. In respect of obtaining housing/accommodation?

7. In respect of accessing health services (e.g. getting access to a GP, access to hospital, access to specialist treatment)?

8. In respect of using transport services?

9. In respect of accessing other public services either at a local or national level?

Self-reported Discrimination

This paper is concerned with two inter-related questions: firstly, what are the characteristics of those most at risk of discrimination according to self-reports? And secondly, does the context matter – are the same groups at risk in different social situations? In answering the second question in particular it is important to bear in mind that involvement in different social contexts, for example accessing health services, education services or the job market, varies across different groups and the rates of discrimination reported apply only to those who participated in this situation at some point over the preceding two years. For example, those who were not involved in the labour market in the last two years were defined as 'not applicable' for the work-related questions. The eligible population therefore varies across the social situations from 100 per cent for 'accessing shop, pubs and restaurants', transport, financial services and other public services, to only 43 per cent for education and 42 per cent for 'looking for work'.

Overall, 12.5 per cent of respondents reported experiencing discrimination in at least one of the domains covered by the questionnaire (see Figure 1). Service-related discrimination was reported by 9 per cent of respondents and work-related discrimination by 7 per cent of respondents. Within the more detailed categories, the highest rate of discrimination reported was in relation to looking for work – 5.8 per cent. Discrimination in the workplace was the next most commonly reported: almost 5 per cent of the eligible population felt discriminated against in this domain.

Figure 1: Rates (%) of Self-reported Discrimination by Social Situation

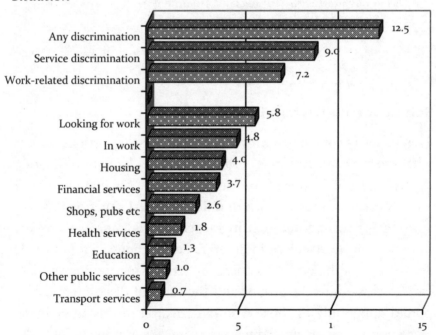

Note: 'Not applicable' are excluded, therefore the Base N differs across the domains (see text)

Within the services domains the highest rates of discrimination were reported in accessing accommodation (4 per cent), financial services (3.7 per cent) and shops, pubs and restaurants (2.6 per cent). The lowest rates of discrimination were reported in accessing education (1.3 per cent) other public services (1 per cent) and using transport services (0.7 per cent).

In the following section the social and demographic characteristics associated with subjective experiences of work-related discrimination and service-discrimination are examined through logistic regression models. Many of the characteristics are covered by anti-discrimination legislation in Ireland such as gender, age, family status, marital status, race/ethnicity, nationality, disability and religion. Two characteristics covered by the equality legislation could not be included in the models – sexual orientation and membership of the Traveller community. Information on respondent's sexual orientation was not collected in the survey, while the number of respondents identifying as Travellers in the ethnicity question was too small for further analysis.[4] The models also include employment status and education level. For the models of work-related discrimination, the characteristics of the job are also controlled but these are not discussed in detail in this chapter (see Russell et al., 2008, p. 18). The section below focuses on the model results and in the concluding section we discuss the extent to which these findings replicate those from studies adopting other methods, for example, studies comparing objective conditions and experimental studies of direct discrimination.

Discrimination at Work and Looking for Work

Women were more likely than men to report they had been discriminated against at work, controlling for a wide range of per-

---

[4] In the follow-on questions respondents could chose sexual orientation as one of the grounds on which they believed they had been discriminated against.

sonal and occupational characteristics. However, men were more likely to report they had been discriminated against in job search.

Age had relatively little impact on either self-reported workplace discrimination or looking for work, so older age groups (45–54 and 55–64 years) were no more likely to report discrimination. In fact, the small number of over-65s in the labour market were much *less* likely to report either discrimination at work or seeking work.

Non-Irish nationals were more than one and a half times as likely as Irish respondents to report discrimination in the workplace and two and half times more likely to report discrimination when looking for work. While the 'raw' percentage of respondents of minority ethnic background reporting work-related discrimination was significantly higher than for White respondents,[5] these differences do not remain significant in the models when other personal and job characteristics are taken into account. There are a number of possible reasons for this non-significance. Firstly, the numbers in the Black, Asian and Other categories are small, and secondly, due to the recent nature of immigration in Ireland there is a strong overlap between non-national and minority ethnic groups. Most respondents from minority ethnic groups experience higher levels of work-related discrimination attached to being a non-Irish national but the models do not indicate an additional penalty for being of Black, Asian or Other ethnicity, once nationality is accounted for. A further test of this was conducted by creating dummy

---

[5] Ten per cent of Black respondents and 17 per cent of Asian respondents reported discrimination at work compared to 5 per cent of White respondents, similarly 18 per cent of Black respondents and 15 per cent of Asian respondents reported discrimination in job search compared to 6 per cent of White respondents. The 'in work' models suggest that Asians may be more likely to experience discrimination in work but the difference is only marginally statistically significant, and is reported in the table as 'same'.

Table 3: Model[1] of Work-related Discrimination: Personal Characteristics

	At Work Odds[2]	Looking for Work Odds
Male	*Reference*	*Reference*
Female	1.38	.59
Irish	*Reference*	*Reference*
Non-Irish	1.54	2.53
White	*Reference*	*Reference*
Black	Same	Same
Asian	Same	Same
'Other'	Same	Same
Catholic	*Reference*	*Reference*
Non-Catholic	1.62	1.40
No disability	*Reference*	*Reference*
Disability	2.76	1.86
Single	*Reference*	*Reference*
Married	.78	0.73
Separated	1.56	Same
No child <15 yrs	*Reference*	*Reference*
Couple child<15 yrs	1.32	Same
Lone parent	Same	Same
Employed	*Reference*	*Reference*
Unemployed	3.14	8.71
Inactive	Same	2.96
Under 25 years	*Reference*	*Reference*
Age 25-44 years	Same	Same
Age 45-54 years	Same	Same
Age 55-64 years	Same	Same
65 + years	0.27	0.13
Primary education	*Reference*	*Reference*
Lower second ed.	Same	0.62
Upper second ed.	Same	0.56
Post-second/Third level	1.62	Same

Note: 1. Logistic regression model. The model also controls for the work characteristics for those in employment: occupation, sector, trade union membership, employment contract (full-time, part-time, self-employed). 2. Odds of less than 1 mean that the group in question is less likely to have experienced discrimination than the reference group. Odds greater than 1 mean they are more likely. All figures reported are statistically significant at the .05 level. 'Same' means that the risk of discrimination does not differ significantly from the reference group.

variables that identified those of Irish nationality who were members of a minority ethnic group – this group was not significantly more likely to report work-related discrimination than White Irish nationals. However, there were only 50 respondents in this category.

Religion is also associated with self-reported discrimination in the workplace. Grouping all those who are not members of the majority Catholic religion together (including those with no religious affiliation), it was found that the non-Catholics were 1.6 times more likely to experience discrimination at work and 1.4 times more likely to report discrimination while looking for work.

People with a disability were almost three times more likely to report discrimination at work than those without a disability and were 1.9 times more likely to report discrimination in job search.

In both job search and at work married people were significantly *less* likely to report discrimination than single people. The small number of separated respondents reported higher levels of discrimination at work than those who were single. In terms of family status, couples with children had somewhat higher odds of experiencing discrimination in work than couples without children. While there was a difference in the 'raw' rates of work discrimination between lone parents and those without children, this difference was not apparent in the model. However the larger group of couples with children were more likely to report discrimination at work than those without children.

Regarding education, those with post-secondary/third level education were more likely to report discrimination in work. In terms of looking for work, those with lower and upper secondary education were less likely to report discrimination than the reference group – those with primary level only. The higher educated did not differ significantly from those with primary education.

Those currently unemployed were significantly more likely to report discrimination 'at work' in the last two years – more than three times as likely as the employed after controlling for their personal characteristics, such as education and age, and job characteristics like sector and occupation. The effect of being unemployed was even more marked with regard to seeking work. Here the unemployed were eight times more likely to report discrimination than the employed who had engaged in job search over the last two years. It is not possible from this data to assess to what extent their unemployment was due to discrimination on the part of employers, but it is clear that a sizeable proportion of this group *felt* they had been discriminated against in seeking work. Discrimination seeking work was also high among those inactive in the labour market.

The models of discrimination at work and discrimination in job hires also control for a range of job characteristics, namely industrial sector, occupational class, trade union membership and employment contract (full-time, part-time, self-employed). These analyses (not shown, see Russell et al. (2008) for details) found that the predictive power of occupational characteristics was considerably weaker than personal characteristics.[6] Self-reports of discrimination were not widely differentiated by occupation or sector, with the same rate occurring across many sectors and occupations when personal characteristics are controlled.[7] The self-employed were less likely to experience discrimination in work due to being their own boss, however they were more likely to report discrimination when looking for work. This latter result suggests that some entry to self-

---

[6] The pseudo R square for personal characteristics was o6o, and when occupational characteristics were added this only increased to o75.

[7] Only those in the Transport and Education sectors reported higher discrimination at work and only those in the Financial services sector reported higher discrimination rate in hiring (out of 11 sectors specified). Across the occupational categories only the unskilled manual respondents had higher rates in the at work model, whereas three of the seven occupational categories had significantly higher rates of self-reported discrimination while looking for work.

employment may be prompted by failure to secure employment. Trade union members were more likely to report discrimination at work, which may be connected to greater awareness of employment rights. It is also possible that trade union members feel discriminated against because of their membership, or that the experience of workplace discrimination may motivate people to become union members. These possible explanations cannot be disentangled with the current data.

Self-reported Discrimination in Accessing Services

Respondents were asked whether they had been discriminated against in accessing seven types of services over the last two years. In the main report the influence of personal characteristics on experiences within each of these social situations was examined through a series of separate models for each domain (Russell et al., 2008). Here we present the results for the overall model, which estimates the likelihood of reporting discrimination in any of the seven domains (Table 4); the results of the individual models are summarised in Table 5.

With the exception of gender, all of the characteristics covered by the equality grounds that were available in the data were found to be significantly linked to the likelihood of reporting discrimination accessing services in the combined model. Within the detailed services domains, women were more likely to say they had been discriminated against in accessing health services, while men were more likely to report discrimination in accessing financial services such as banking and insurance (Table 5).

Young people aged 18 to 24 years (the reference group) were much more likely than all other age groups to report discrimination while accessing services. The detailed models showed that this effect was strongest in financial services, housing, and shops, pubs and restaurants.

Table 4: Model of Services Discrimination in Last Two Years

Group	Odds
Male	*Reference*
Female	Same
18 – 24 years	*Reference*
25 – 44 years	0.67
45 – 64 years	0.45
65+ years	0.31
White	*Reference*
Black	2.70
Asian	Same
Other ethnic group	1.71
Irish	*Reference*
Non-Irish	1.34
Catholic	*Reference*
Not Catholic	1.60
No disability	*Reference*
Disability	3.26
Single	*Reference*
Separated	1.34
Married	0.75
No child <15 years	*Reference*
Couple child <15 years	1.31
Lone Parent child <15 years	1.85
Primary Education	*Reference*
Secondary level	Same
Post-second Level	1.21
Employed	*Reference*
Unemployed	1.39
Inactive	1.43

Note: All figures reported are statistically significant at the .05 level. 'Same' means that the risk of discrimination does not differ significantly from the reference group. Odds less than 1 imply a lower risk than reference group. Not Catholic includes those of no religion, who also report a higher rate of discrimination relative to Catholic.

Table 5: High Risk Groups by Service Domain

Domain	Groups
Housing	Non-Irish nationals, Black and 'Other' ethnicity, no religion, lower education, unemployed, economically inactive, people with disabilities, lone parents, parents, non-married
Health	Women, minority religious groups, 25-64 years, people with disabilities, separated, unemployed, inactive, parents
Shops, pubs, restaurants	Young people, minority ethnic groups, non-Irish, people with disabilities, unemployed and economically inactive
Financial Institutions	Young people, men, Black ethnicity, non-Irish nationals, people with disabilities, not married, graduates, no religion, minority religious groups
Transport	People with disabilities, Black or Asian ethnic groups, non-Irish nationals, minority religious groups, economically inactive, respondents with children, including lone parents
Education	People aged 18-44, other Christian, unemployed, economically inactive, parents with children under 15 years
Other public services	Other Christian, no religion, people with disabilities, economically inactive, those with children under 15 years including lone parents

Note: These results are taken from regression models that control for all the characteristics outlined in Table 4. The full model results are available in Russell et al., 2008.

The model results for ethnicity show that Black respondents had a significantly higher risk of services discrimination than White respondents, even when other characteristics were held constant (including nationality). The highest relative rate of self-reported discrimination for those of Black ethnicity was in relation to shops, pubs or restaurants, where this group were almost five times more likely to experience discrimination than White respondents. Those of 'Other' ethnic background were also more likely to report greater discrimination accessing services in the combined model (Table 4).

Non-Irish nationals were 1.3 times more likely to report discrimination accessing services than Irish nationals, suggesting that nationality has a less pronounced effect in this domain than in the labour market as seen above. Within the service categories, nationality had the greatest impact in relation to using transport services.

Respondents who were members of minority religious groups or had no religious affiliation were more likely to report service discrimination than Catholic respondents. This effect was significant in all seven service domains examined.

Disability was the characteristic most strongly associated with self-reported discrimination in services. People with disabilities were 3.3 times more likely to report such discrimination than those without a disability. The rate of discrimination for this group was highest in transport services and health services, and was also significant in all service domains except education.

Marital status and family status also proved significant. The married group was *less likely* to perceive discrimination in services than single people, as was the case for work-related discrimination. The context was significant here: marriage was irrelevant for education, health, transport or other public services, but was particularly 'advantageous' in terms of access to housing and to a lesser extent accessing financial services, and pubs, shops or restaurants. The separated group were more likely to report discrimination than those who were single. Respondents with children were significantly more likely to report service discrimination in the combined model, with lone parents reporting the highest level of discrimination among the family status groups. Family status was particularly relevant in the financial service and education models and was not significant in the health service domain.

Overall then, the groups identified as needing protection from discrimination under equality legislation were indeed more likely to report that they had experienced discrimination in accessing services and/or in the labour market over the preceding two years. It is noticeable that some groups experienced discrimination in a wide variety of domains. For example, people with disabilities were found to be at higher risk of discrimination in both work-related and all but one of the service domains (except education). Similarly, non-Irish nationals were more likely than Irish nationals to report discrimination in four service domains and both work-related domains. For other groups discrimination was more context-specific, for example young people were particularly likely to report discrimination in the use of financial services and shops, pubs and restaurants. In the concluding section we will discuss how these results correspond to findings from other studies in the Irish context. Before concluding, the impact of perceived discrimination and the actions taken in response to discrimination are discussed briefly.

Impact of Discrimination

Of those experiencing discrimination, 26 per cent said it had a serious or very serious impact on their lives. The impact of discrimination was found to vary across social groups and also depended on the context. Workplace discrimination and discrimination accessing housing were found to have a more serious impact. The former result is likely to arise because the domain of employment is particularly important to individuals' quality of life and mental well-being. Employment also represents a social situation where there is an ongoing set of relationships and interactions, whereas in other domains interactions are more likely to be of a one-off or intermittent nature. A denial of employment due to discrimination can also have serious financial consequences. A denial of housing could also have significant consequences for individuals' quality of life.

A statistical model of the characteristics associated with a more severe impact found that people with disabilities were most likely to report serious impact, which may be linked to their higher likelihood of experiencing discrimination across multiple domains. The unemployed were also significantly more likely to respond that discrimination had a serious impact on their lives when other personal characteristics were held constant.

Responses to Discrimination

Sixty per cent of those who self-reported discrimination took no action. The most common form of action taken was verbal, with 26 per cent saying they had taken such action. A further 4 per cent made a written response, with only 6 per cent making a formal response by making an official complaint or taking a legal action. This result suggests that the cases that make it to the Equality Tribunal, the Labour Court or other legal arena represent a very small fraction of all cases of discrimination. 'In work' discrimination was most likely to prompt action; discrimination while looking for work was least likely to have been responded to.

Regarding taking action, the analysis shows that in many cases the social groups who report experiencing the highest levels of discrimination are the least likely to take action. Responding to discrimination requires a range of resources such as language skills, confidence and knowledge of one's rights and entitlements. It appears that more marginalised groups who are subject to higher levels of discrimination may also lack some of these resources.

Conclusions: Do Self-reports of Discrimination Confirm Evidence from Other Sources?

The self-reported data from the QNHS Equality Module based on a nationally representative sample of the Irish population suggest that 7 per cent of labour market participants experienced discrimination over a two-year period, while 9 per cent of the population report discrimination accessing services. The results represent an important first benchmark on the distribution of perceived discrimination across social groups and within different social contexts, and provide a basis for tracking changes in perceived discrimination over time. Self-report data alone cannot establish incidence and distribution of discrimination but can be used to corroborate other sources of evidence for Ireland. A key issue, then, is how far the distribution of self-reported discrimination in the labour market and services is in agreement with other research results.

The greater likelihood of women to report discrimination 'at work' is consistent with analyses of working conditions and labour market experiences, which show that women are disadvantaged relative to men, for example in relation to pay when other human capital characteristics are controlled (McGuinness et al., 2009; Russell and Gannon, 2002; Russell et al., 2005; see Gregory, this volume, for international evidence), and occupational positions (Russell et al., 2009; O'Connor, 1998; Fahey et al., 2000). However, the size of the gender difference is perhaps smaller than these studies on objective conditions would suggest. This may be because, in objective labour market inequality, structural inequalities such as gender segregation also play a role and these are not experienced as direct personal discrimination.

High rates of self-reported discrimination among people with disabilities in the labour market and in accessing services is also consistent with previous Irish research, which found that people with disabilities are significantly disadvantaged in the labour market and in other spheres such as poverty and social participation (see Gannon and Nolan, this volume). Gannon and Nolan (2004) found that people with disabilities were more likely to be unemployed or outside the labour market, holding other characteristics constant, and were disadvantaged in terms of earnings (Gannon and Nolan, 2005). There is also evidence of prejudicial attitudes towards people with disabilities (CSO, 2010),

Research on objective labour market conditions also show that non-Irish nationals are significantly disadvantaged in the labour market in terms of unemployment risks, occupational position and wages, even when factors such as educational level, labour market experience, length of time in country and language ability are controlled (O'Connell and McGinnity, 2008; Barrett et al., 2006; Barrett and McCarthy, 2007). McGinnity et al. (this volume, and 2009) also found direct evidence of discrimination against non-Irish nationals in recruitment through a field experiment among Irish employers. The experiment found that job applicants from German, Asian and African backgrounds were only half as likely to be called to interview as Irish candidates.

High levels of self-reported discrimination in services among minority ethnic groups in Ireland were also reported by McGinnity et al. (2006) and in smaller non-statistically representative surveys of ethnic minority groups (e.g. Amnesty International Ireland, 2001). O'Connell and McGinnity (2008) also found that Black respondents were significantly more likely to experience unemployment and to occupy lower level occupational positions when education, work experience and nationality are controlled. The insignificance of ethnicity in the work-related discrimination models, despite the high raw rates of self-reported discrimination, may therefore be attributable to the methodological issues discussed (primarily small number of cases), rather than accurately reflecting the underlying reality.

While there is a strong level of correspondence in the results of the self-report survey and studies using other methods to investigate inequality and discrimination, there are nevertheless a number of important inconsistencies (in addition to the differences in strength of effects outlined above).

Firstly, studies of income, labour market and social inclusion show that graduates are objectively advantaged (for example, O'Connell et al., 2004; Russell et al., 2010) but they report higher discrimination at work and accessing services. It is likely that higher self-reports of discrimination among this group arise from a greater awareness of rights, higher expectations about equal treatment, and a greater propensity to report discrimination to a third party. Results from other research also show that the highly educated are more likely to self-report discrimination (e.g. McGinnity et al., 2006; EUMC, 2006).

Secondly, the QNHS module finds that older people have low levels of self-reported discrimination in both the labour market and services despite evidence of ageism in attitude surveys (O'Connor and Dowds, 2003) and poorer outcomes in some service areas, e.g. financial exclusion (Russell and Maitre, forthcoming) and health care (McGlone, 2005). Evidence on objective conditions of older people in the labour market varies depending on the outcome examined. Among those in employment, older workers tend to occupy higher occupational positions (Russell and Fahey, 2004). Wages also increase with age, due to increased seniority and experience (e.g. Barrett et al., 2000). Similarly, the rates of unemployment tend to be lower among older workers. However, a number of studies have shown that, once unemployed, older people have more difficulty re-entering employment (e.g. O'Connell et al., 2009). Experimental studies in other countries have also found direct evidence of discrimination in recruitment on the basis of age (Rich, this volume).

These research results suggest that, other things being equal, older people are less likely to identify their treatment as being discriminatory. This may partly be due to a lack of awareness of rights: in the QNHS Equality Module, 28 per cent of those aged over 65 years said they had no knowledge of their rights under Irish equality law, compared to 20 per cent of the whole population.

Where the self-reported results are not corroborated by other sources of evidence, as in these cases, it is important to consider possible biases in responses caused by cultural factors, differential resources or other issues which make some groups more or less likely to identify discriminatory treatment.

Policy Implications

The results of this study suggest that accessing financial services and housing, along with recruitment and the workplace, are areas that may require particular monitoring for discriminatory practices. In the case of work-related discrimination, the response of the unemployed and the economically inactive, non-Irish nationals (including minority ethnic migrants) and people with disabilities suggest that these groups are particularly at risk. In relation to services, disabled people, non-Irish nationals and minority ethnic groups reported greater likelihood of consistently experiencing discrimination. The finding that some of the groups who most commonly report discrimination are the least likely to take action indicates the potential benefit of proactive third party interventions, such as information campaigns, advocacy and legal supports, along with initiatives by employers and service providers to implement good practice. These strategies are also important to raise awareness of rights among groups who appear to under-report discrimination, for example, older people and those with lower levels of education.

The Equality Module is due to be repeated by the CSO in the fourth quarter of 2010. This will provide a valuable opportunity to track changes in perceived discrimination over time. It will also provide evidence to address questions of whether the economic downturn since 2008 has led to increased discrimination in general, and against certain groups in particular (e.g. migrants, ethnic minorities and those with disabilities). This changed context makes the continued collection of equality relevant data all the more important.

References

Amnesty International Ireland (2001) *Racism in Ireland: The Views of Black and Ethnic Minorities*. Dublin: Amnesty International (Irish Section).

Barrett, A. Bergin, A. and Duffy, D. (2006) 'The Labour Market Characteristics and Labour Market Impacts of Immigrants in Ireland', *The Economic and Social Review*, Spring, pp. 1-26.

Barrett, A., Callan, T, Doris, A., O'Neill, D, Russell, H, Sweetman, O. and McBride, J. (2000), *How Unequal? Men and Women in the Irish Labour Market*, Dublin: Oak Tree Press.

Barrett, A. and McCarthy, Y. (2007); 'Immigrants in a Booming Economy: Analysing their Earnings and Welfare Dependence', *Labour*, Vol. 21, No. 4.

Blank, R.M., Dabady, M. and Citro, C.F. (eds.) (2004). *Measuring Racial Discrimination*. Washington DC: The National Academies Press.

Bond, L., McGinnity, F. and Russell, H. (2010) 'Introduction: Making Equality Count' in L. Bond, F. McGinnity and H. Russell (eds.) *Making Equality Count: Irish and International Research Measuring Equality and Discrimination* Dublin: The Liffey Press.

Central Statistics Office (2010) *National Disability Survey 2006, Volume 2*. Dublin: Stationery Office.

Darity, W. (2010) 'Racism and Colorism in Post-Racial Societies' in L. Bond, F. McGinnity and H. Russell (eds.) *Making Equality Count: Irish and International Research Measuring Equality and Discrimination* Dublin: The Liffey Press.

Darity, W. and Mason, P. (1998). 'Evidence on Discrimination in Employment: Codes of Color, Codes of Gender', *The Journal of Economic Perspectives*, Vol. 12, No. 2, pp. 63-90.

European Monitoring Centre on Racism and Xenophobia (2006) *Migrants' Experiences of Racism and Xenophobia in 12 EU Member States: Pilot Study*, Vienna: EUMC

Fahey, T., Smyth, E. and Russell, H. (2000) 'Gender Equality, Fertility Decline and Labour Market Patterns among Women in Ireland', in B. Nolan, P.J. O'Connelll and C.T. Whelan (eds.) *From Bust to Boom?: The Irish Experience of Growth and Inequality*. Dublin: IPA.

Gannon, B. and Nolan, B. (2004). *Disability and Labour Market Participation*, Dublin: The Equality Authority.

Gannon, B. and Nolan, B. (2005). *Disability and Social Inclusion in Ireland*, Dublin: National Disability Authority and The Equality Authority.

Gannon, B. and Nolan, B. (2010) 'Disability and Social Inclusion in Ireland' in L. Bond, F. McGinnity and H. Russell (eds.) *Making Equality Count: Irish and International Research Measuring Equality and Discrimination* Dublin: The Liffey Press.

Garner, S. (2004). *Racism in the Irish Experience*. London: Pluto Press.

Gregory, M. (2010) 'Assessing Unequal Treatment: Gender and Pay' in L. Bond, F. McGinnity and H. Russell (eds.) *Making Equality Count: Irish and International Research Measuring Equality and Discrimination* Dublin: The Liffey Press.

Kessler, R.C., Mickelson, K.D. and Williams, D.R. (1999) 'The Prevalence, Distribution, and Mental Health Correlates of Perceived Discrimination in the United States', *Journal of Health and Social Behavior*, Vol. 40, No. 3. pp. 208-230.

Loury, G.C. (2002) *The Anatomy of Racial Inequality*, Cambridge MA: Harvard University Press.

McGinnity, F., O'Connell, P.J., Quinn, E. and Williams, J. (2006). *Migrants' Experience of Racism and Discrimination in Ireland*: *Survey Report*, Dublin: The Economic and Social Research Institute.

McGinnity, F., Nelson, J., Lunn, P. and Quinn, E. (2009) *Discrimination in Recruitment: Evidence from a field experiment*. Dublin: The Equality Authority and The Economic and Social Research Institute.

McGinnity, F., Nelson, J., Lunn, P.D. and Quinn, E. (2010) 'Are Eamon and Eithne More Employable than Hardeep and Heike? Evidence from a Field Experiment in Ireland' in L. Bond, F. McGinnity and H. Russell (eds.) *Mak-*

ing Equality Count: Irish and International Research Measuring Equality and Discrimination Dublin: The Liffey Press.

McGlone, E (2005) 'Ageism in the Health and Social Services Sector in Ireland', in Y. McGivern (ed.) *From Ageism to Age Equality: Addressing the Challenges, Conference Proceedings*, Dublin: National Council for Ageing and Older People.

O'Connell, P.J. and McGinnity, F. (2008). *Immigrants at Work: Ethnicity and Nationality in the Irish Labour Market*, Dublin: The Equality Authority and The Economic and Social Research Institute.

O'Connell, P.J., McGuinness, S., Kelly, E. and Walsh, J.R. (2009) *National Profiling of the Unemployed in Ireland*, Dublin: ESRI Research Series No. 10.

O'Connell, P.J., Russell, H., Williams, J. and Blackwell, S. (2004) *The Changing Workplace: A Survey of Employees' Views and Experiences*, Dublin: NCPP.

O'Connor, P. (1998) *Emerging Voices: Women in Contemporary Irish Society*, Dublin: IPA.

O'Connor, P. and Dowds, L. (2003) Ageism and Attitudes to Older People in the Republic of Ireland: Report of ARK Survey.

Pager, D. and Shepherd, H. (2008) 'The Sociology of Discrimination: Racial Discrimination in Employment, Housing, Credit and Consumer Markets', *Annual Review of Sociology*, 34, pp. 181-209.

Rich, J. (2010) 'Measuring Discrimination: What do Field Experiments of Markets Tell Us' in L. Bond, F. McGinnity and H. Russell (eds.) *Making Equality Count: Irish and International Research Measuring Equality and Discrimination* Dublin: The Liffey Press.

Russell, H. and Fahey, T. (2004). *Ageing and Labour Market Participation*. Dublin: The Equality Authority.

Russell, H. and Gannon, B. (2002). 'The Gender Wage Gap in Ireland', *Impact Evaluation of the European Employment Strategy in Ireland*, Dublin: Department of Enterprise, Trade and Employment.

Russell, H., Smyth, E. and O'Connell, P.J. (2005). *Degrees of Equality: Gender Differentials among Recent Graduates*, Dublin: The Economic and Social Research Institute.

Russell, H., Quinn, E., O'Riain, R. and McGinnity, F. (2008) *The Experience of Discrimination in Ireland: Analysis of the QNHS Equality Module*, Dublin: The Equality Authority and The Economic and Social Research Institute.

Russell, H. McGinnity, F., Callan, T. and Keane, C. (2009) *A Woman's Place: Female Participation in the Irish Labour Market*, Dublin: The Equality Authority and The Economic and Social Research Institute.

Russell, H. Maitre, B. and Nolan, B. (2010) *Monitoring Poverty Trends in Ireland 2004-2007: Key Issues for Children, People of Working Age and Older People*. Dublin: ESRI Research Series, Number 17.

Russell, H. and Maitre, B. (forthcoming) 'Over-indebtedness and Financial Exclusion in Ireland: Evidence from EU SILC 2008', Dublin: The Economic and Social Research Institute.

Steele, C. (1997) 'A Threat in the Air: How Stereotypes Shape Intellectual Identity and Performance' *American Psychologist*, Vol. 52, No. 2, pp. 613-29.

Chapter 3

Measuring Discrimination: What Do Field Experiments of Markets Tell Us?

Judith Rich

What are field experiments of markets and what does this research tell us about discriminatory behaviour and practices? Field experiments do not aim to draw national conclusions and generalisations about the extent (or not) of discrimination in the way that wage regression analysis does. What they do aim to do is to detect discrimination within an area of markets that they survey. In this chapter some brief background information on field experiments is provided for those unfamiliar with this work. Then the findings of field experiments are discussed in two parts: field experiments conducted over the period 1966 to 2000; field experiments conducted over the period 2000 to 2010. Finally, some comments are made about innovations to the testing procedure undertaken in these recent field experiments.

General Background to Field Experiments

In the UK in 1967, field experiments were designed to assess the efficacy of anti-discrimination law, specifically to assess the efficacy of the Race Relations Act at the time. The UN had approached the British Government requesting them to conduct an assessment of the Race Relations Act as, in 1966, it did not cover transactions that occurred in housing and labour markets.

Daniel (1968) devised an approach that comprised three parts: a survey of employers, a survey of employees and in-situ tests. These in-situ tests sent actors to apply for jobs and to enquire about renting or buying a flat or house. These types of field experiments are now called in-person tests or audits. The actors were sent in matched pairs where one tester was always of British origin and the other was either a Hungarian or Asian/West Indian immigrant. Daniel found high levels of discrimination against Hungarians and Asian/West Indians. The UK parliamentary papers, Hansard, reported these findings and Daniels' research was influential in passing amendments to the Race Relations Act.

Critical evaluation of these initial tests raised the issue of the motivation of the testers that were involved. It was argued that the researcher could not guarantee that these testers were consciously or subconsciously aiding the researcher by actually demonstrating that discrimination existed. In response to this criticism, Jowell and Prescott Clarke (1970) devised correspondence tests (written tests) where two matched curriculum vitae (CVs) were sent in application for advertised job vacancies.

So three types of approaches have been developed for field experiment research. First there are audits or in-person tests, where carefully matched testers (actors but more usually undergraduate students) apply in person for jobs in the labour market, for rental accommodation or to purchase a house or flat in the housing market, and in the product market for goods or services. In applying for jobs, for example, the matching of applicants controls for all aspects of an individual that would affect their work productivity such as schooling, work experience, training, socio-economic background etc., as well as their personal appearance such as attractiveness, height, weight, and so on. Testers are trained in job specific requirements and interview technique for the labour market tests, in presentation and enquiry technique for the housing market tests, and so on. The end result is that the matched pair of testers are to all intents and purposes presenting for a market transaction as identical except for the basis which the researcher is investigating such as race, ethnicity, sex, age, sexual orientation or disability. In the second type of approach, audits or in-person tests are conducted over the telephone where once again the paired applicants are matched.

Third, there are correspondence or written tests. For correspondence tests in the labour market, curriculum vitae (résumés) are constructed which carefully match for socio-economic background, educational qualifications, work experience, hobbies and interests so that, once again, the applicants are identical except for the basis which the researcher is investigating such as race, ethnicity, sex, age, sexual orientation or disability. These CVs are usually vetted by professionals in the occupations to be tested, as well as by others involved in hiring such as employment agencies. Tests in the housing market involve sending a written enquiry, usually by email, in response to a flat or house advertised for rent or sale with relevant information for decision-making on the part of the landlord/owner/real estate manager controlled so that the researcher can select the basis for investigation of any possible differential treatment of applicants.

The General Findings from Field Experiments of Markets 1966 to 2000

Riach and Rich (2002; 2004) surveyed over 100 field experiments which had been conducted between 1966 and 2000 using the three approaches described above. The general findings from these experiments which have investigated differential treatment in nine countries on the basis of race, ethnicity, sex, age or disability in labour, housing and product markets, are presented in this section. Table 1 shows only the results of these studies reported as *net discrimination*, where net discrimination

Table 1: Broad Range of Results for Net Discrimination for Studies Conducted between 1966 and 2000[1]

Country of Test	Market and Basis of Test	Minority Group	Range of Net Discrimination[2,3] %
Australia	LM Race	Vietnamese	27.4***
Australia	LM Race	Greek	8.8**
Australia	LM Sex	Female	-5.6 to 16.1*
Austria	LM Sex	Female	-50.0** to 18.7
Belgium	LM Race	Moroccan	21.0** to 50.5***
Canada	LM Race	West Indian	39.1***
England	LM Race	Asian/West Indian	24.0*** to 50.0***
England	LM Disability	Disabled	33.0*** to 37.6***
England	HM Race	Asian/West Indian	12.4* to 60.1*
Germany	LM Race	Turkish	18.9***
Netherlands	LM Race	Moroccan	41.6*** to 44.4***
Netherlands	LM Disability	Disabled	24.0***
Spain	LM Race	Moroccan	42.3** to 47.0***
USA	LM Race	African-American	2.8 to 70.8***
USA	LM Race	Hispanic	21.4*** to 25.1***
USA	LM Sex	Female	-75.0** to 75.0***
USA	LM Age	Older	31.4***
USA	HM Race	African-American	13.1* to 70.0*
USA	HM Race	Hispanic	4.0* to 47.0*

Note: 1. Details of these studies available in Riach and Rich (2002). 2. Chi-squared tests were conducted on the response rates and the results are indicated as * significant at the 0.05 level; ** significant at the 0.01 level; *** significant at the 0.001 level. 3. A minus sign indicates discrimination against the majority applicant.

is defined as the responses where only the majority applicant was invited to interview (or to view a rental property) *minus* the responses where only the minority applicant was invited to interview (or to view a rental property). The net discrimination levels reported in Table 1 refer to the *range* of net discrimination that has been found across a number of studies that have been conducted by various researchers in the respective countries. Statistical significance is indicated by asterisks and usually refers to a chi-square test. A finding of negative net discrimination indicates that, overall, the *majority* applicant was discriminated against. For example, in a study on the basis of sex, a finding of negative net discrimination means that males were discriminated against. Full details of the results and further information for each separate study discussed in this section can been found in Riach and Rich (2002).

In the USA the tests on race in the labour market have found discrimination against African-Americans in a range 2.8 per cent to 70 per cent (Riach and Rich, 2002: F497). Why would it be 2.8 per cent, a very low level, to very high levels? This is because when researchers use written tests, the names of African-Americans may not be distinct and so at the initial stage of the hiring process the employer reading a CV is unlikely to be able to recognise the race of the applicant. On the other hand, if all the stages of hiring are tested by the researcher, from the initial stage of vetting of a CV or résumé through to actually going to an interview, then discrimination may be detected when the race of the applicant becomes apparent to the employer. There have also been studies testing for discrimination against Hispanics in hiring decisions which have found a range of net discrimination between 21 per cent and 25 per cent (Riach and Rich, 2002: F497). Studies of discrimination against African-Americans and Hispanics have been conducted in the housing market as well, and these studies also found discrimination against both groups when enquiring to rent or buy flats or houses: levels of net discrimination between 13.1 per cent and 70.0 per cent for African-Americans and levels of net discrimination of 4.0 per cent to 47 per cent for Hispanics (Riach and Rich, 2002: F512). Continuing with the studies in the USA, tests for hiring discrimination on the basis of sex have recorded net discrimination levels of -75 per cent to +75 per cent. These studies found that the level of discrimination against men applying to female-dominated jobs is approximately twice that experienced by women applying to male-dominated jobs (Riach and Rich, 2002: F501-F502). Discrimination has also been recorded in the US labour market against older applicants for employment, a level of 31.4 per cent (Riach and Rich, 2002: F506). There have also been a few studies conducted in the US, not reported in Table 1, testing for discrimination in the product market. These have found that females, minorities, and older individuals pay more for cars and car insurance (Ayres 1991; Ayres and Siegelman, 1995).

In England, there have been tests in both the labour and housing markets on the basis of race (Asian/West Indian) and in the labour market on the basis of disability, all finding discrimination against the minority applicant (Riach and Rich, 2002: F489-90, F495, F506, F512). The studies of discrimination in the labour market recorded levels of net discrimination between 24.0 per cent and 50.0 per cent for Asian/West Indians enquiring for jobs. The studies of discrimination in the housing market recorded levels of net discrimination of 12.4 per cent to 60.1 per cent for Asian/West Indians enquiring to rent or buy flats or houses. The studies of discrimination of disabled individuals applying for jobs recorded levels of net discrimination between 33.0 per cent and 37.6 per cent.

West Indians were found to be discriminated against in hiring in Canada; a level of net discrimination of 39.1 per cent was found in these tests (Riach and Rich, 2002: F500). Moroccans were found to be discriminated against in Belgium (levels of 21.0 per cent to 50.5 per cent), the Netherlands (levels of 41.6 per cent to 44.4 per cent) and Spain (levels of 42.3 per cent to 47.0 per cent) (Riach and Rich, 2002: F495). In Germany, when minority applicants were given Turkish names a level of discrimination of 18.9 per cent was recorded (Riach and Rich, 2002: F495). Vietnamese and Greeks were found to be discriminated against in Australia (a level of net discrimination of, respectively 27.4 per cent and 8.8 per cent), as were females for higher level, higher paying jobs (a level of net discrimination of 16.1 per cent) (Riach and Rich, 2002: F500, F501). All the studies discussed above recorded statistically significant levels of discrimination against the minority applicant

It is pertinent to mention that research conducted by the International Labour Office (ILO) confirmed that the vast majority of discrimination detected in hiring occurred at the initial stage of vetting the CVs of applicants (Riach and Rich, 2002: F494). This is particularly relevant to field experiments using the written approach as these studies are usually confined to testing only the initial hiring stage where applicants are assessed solely on the CV that they have sent to an employer. The ILO findings mean that these written approaches are testing hiring decisions in the labour market where the majority of discrimination practices occur.

In summary, these tests found that overwhelmingly for minorities and women access to jobs was restricted, access to housing was restricted, and they paid more for products. These tests also show us other dimensions of differential treatment as the testers record aspects of the interview with the researchers. The following have been found at interview: differences in the time spent at interviews; and differences in treatment at or before interview such as treated courteously or not, seating arrangements for the applicant, etc. There were cases where the job had been filled but the minority applicant was offered another job which was lower paid or lower status, whereas the majority applicant in this situation was offered a better paid or higher level position. Steering in housing markets was found where the African-

American was steered towards African-American neighbourhoods and the White was steered towards white neighbourhoods.

How does the body of research just presented fit in with more
conventional methods of research? These field experiments complement a vast body of research which has found for minorities
and women that earnings are lower (wage regression analysis),
that unemployment is higher, that employment is restricted (occupational segregation studies) and that promotion is limited
(cohort studies, some using survival hazard rate models).

Findings from Field Experiments of Markets 2000 to 2010

I now turn to discuss the studies which have been conducted
over the last decade, 2000 to 2010. There has been a quiet revolution in academia with many more researchers now investigating discrimination in markets using an experimental approach.
Over the last decade there have been just over twenty such studies of discrimination. Many of these more recent studies have
used a variation on the written approach sending multiple CVs
in application for a job vacancy. Table 2 shows the results for the
majority of these studies reported as net discrimination where,
as in Table 1, the net discrimination levels reported refer to the
range of net discrimination that has been found across a number
of studies that have been conducted by various researchers in
the respective countries. However, not all the studies can be
placed in Table 2. Some of the recent experiments which have
sent multiple applications to a job advertisement do not report
the level of net discrimination, while others do. All these studies
report the callback rate defined as the number of positive responses to an applicant (such as asked to submit more information or invited to interview) as a proportion of total applications
(CV submitted) made by the applicant. Table 3 reports the call-

back rates that have been found. It should be noted that some duplication of the studies reported occurs with their results reported as net discrimination in Table 2 and callback rates in Table 3. This is the case for studies conducted in Germany, Great Britain, Ireland and the USA. Full details of the results and further information for each separate study discussed in this section can been found in Rich and Judge (2010).

In the labour market there have been studies conducted of hiring testing for discrimination on the basis of race sex, age and obesity. In the housing market there have been studies conducted of offers to rent or view accommodation testing for discrimination on the basis of race and sexual orientation. In the product market there has been further research on the impact of race, gender and age on pricing outcomes in transactions. All these experimental studies report finding statistically significant levels of discrimination.

Table 2 reports net discrimination rates found in studies from seven countries – Great Britain, France, Germany, Greece, Ireland, Sweden, and the USA – of hiring in the labour market testing for discrimination on the basis of race. The results show ongoing significant levels of discrimination: Africans in Ireland face a net discrimination rate of 48.2 per cent, African-Americans in the USA a level of 29.6 per cent, Albanians in Greece a range of 24.2 per cent to 65.7 per cent, Asians in Great Britain and in Ireland a level of 35 per cent, those of Middle-Eastern background in Sweden a range of 28.9 per cent to 44.6 per cent, Moroccans in France a range of 40.9 per cent to 54.4 per cent, and Turkish applicants in Germany a level of 10.1 per cent.

Table 2 also includes English results on discrimination in hiring on the basis of sex, studies from England, France and Spain which examined age discrimination in the labour market, and Swedish results on discrimination on the basis of obesity.

Table 2: Broad Range of Results for Net Discrimination for Studies Conducted between 2000 and 2010[1]

Country of Test	Market and Basis of Test	Ethnic or Minority Group	Range of Net Discrimination[2,3] %
Great Britain	LM Race	Black Minority Ethnicity	35.0[*]
England	LM Sex	Female	-43.1[***] to 23.1[**]
England	LM Age	Older	-29.6 to 59.6[***]
France	LM Age	Older	58.1[***]
France	LM Race	Moroccan	40.9[***] to 54.4[***]
Germany	LM Race	Turkish	10.1[*]
Greece	LM Race	Albanian	24.2[**] to 65.7[***]
Ireland	LM Race	African	48.1[**]
Ireland	LM Race	Asian	35.3[*]
Spain	LM Age	Older	64.5***
Sweden	LM Race	Middle Eastern	28.9*** to 44.6***
Sweden	LM Obesity	Obese	0 to 42.9**
Sweden	HM Race	Middle Eastern	-9.5* to 34.5*
Sweden	HM Sexual Orientation	Homosexual	19.9*
USA	LM Race	African-American	29.6*

Note: 1. Details of these studies are available in Rich and Judge (2010). 2. Chi-squared tests were conducted on the response rates and the results are indicated as as * significant at the 0.05 level; ** significant at the 0.01 level; *** significant at the 0.001 level. 3. A minus sign indicates discrimination against the majority applicant.

On the basis of sex: in England studies found a range of -43.1 per cent to +23.1 per cent, a level of discrimination against men applying to female-dominated jobs at a level nearly twice that experienced by women applying to male-dominated jobs. The results found on the basis of age were: in England a range of 28.8 per cent to 59.6 per cent, in France a level of 58.1 per cent, in Spain a level of 64.5 per cent, with the very high level of net discrimination recorded against older applicants amongst the highest recorded by these experiments. On the basis of obesity in Sweden a range 0 per cent to 42.9 per cent against the obese applicant was found, where the researcher signalled obesity by attaching a digitally enhanced photo of an individual who was made to look obese to one CV while using the normal photo of the same individual, who had been judged to be attractive, for the matched CV. All the above findings of discrimination were statistically significant.

Turning now to the recent tests in the housing market: in the USA tests in 2000 found that for housing inspections African Americans were discriminated against at a statistically significant level, but Hispanics were not. (It was not possible to report net discrimination levels for these tests). In Sweden there have been tests conducted in the housing market controlling for race and sexual orientation. Men with a Middle Eastern background as compared to Swedish women were discriminated against when invited to view accommodation at a level of 34.5 per cent. However men with a Middle Eastern background as compared to Swedish men were preferred on invitations to view accommodation, a level of net discrimination of -9.5 per cent was recorded. Testing for discrimination on the basis of sexual orientation in Sweden found homosexuals were discriminated against when they applied to rent or purchase a property, a level of net discrimination 19.9 per cent.

In the USA in the product market tests again found that women, older people and minorities, paid more for sport cards than did young white men. That is, controlling for bargaining method, mannerisms and technique by training, when individuals other than young white men enquired to buy sport cards, they were invariably quoted higher prices.

Table 3: Broad Range of Results for Callback Rates for Studies Conducted Between 2000 and 2010[1]

Country of Test	Market and Basis of Test	Ethnic or Minority Group	Callback Rate %
Australia	LM Race	White	35
		Chinese	21
		Italian	32
		Middle Eastern	22
Great Britain	LM Race	Black Minority Ethnicity	6.2
		White	10.7
Germany	LM Race	Turkish	32.5
		White	41.8
Ireland	LM Race	African	11.1
		White	27.2
USA	LM Race	African-American	6.5
		White	9.7

Note: 1. Details of these studies are available in Rich and Judge (2010).

Studies that recorded callback rates to applicants also report differential treatment. Table 3 indicates that majority applicants received statistically significant greater rates of callback. White applicants received a greater level of positive responses to job applications than, Chinese or Middle-Eastern applicants in Australia, Turkish applicants in Germany, black minority ethnic applicants in Great Britain, African applicants in Ireland and African-Americans in the USA. The researchers in these studies highlight a different outcome than net discrimination. They draw attention to the average number of applications a job candidate needs to make to achieve a positive response from an employer. They then investigate for differences to their various applicants in this outcome. For example, the study conducted in the USA found that to obtain a positive response from an employer, a white applicant needed to apply to 10 (1/9.7) jobs whereas an African-American applicant needed to apply to 15 (1/6.5) jobs. Similar results were found in the study conducted in Great Britain where a white person needed to apply to 9 jobs whereas a black or ethnic minority person needed to apply to 16 jobs to receive an invitation to interview.

In summary the studies conducted between 2000 and 2010 found access to jobs was restricted for racial minorities, women, older and obese individuals, access to housing was restricted for racial minorities and homosexuals and that racial minorities, women and older individuals paid more for products. A caveat needs to be added as the housing market tests conducted in 2000 in the USA found that net discrimination had declined for both minority groups since the last tests had been conducted in 1989.

General Comments on Field Experiments and Recent Innovations

We should remember that these latest findings are all in an era where countries have anti-discrimination legislation making it illegal to discriminate against individuals on various bases and there has been much discussion about discrimination in the public arena. So, it is rather alarming that these tests over the last decade report the same findings as those conducted over the period 1966 to 2000. We should also recognise that one of the impacts of anti-discrimination legislation is that no sensible employer would behave in a very overt fashion if they engaged in discriminatory practices. The research of social psychologists (Ellemers and Barreto, 2009) indicates that there has been a shift in discriminatory practices with these practices becoming far more subtle and much more difficult for individuals to detect. This means it would be extremely difficult for an individual to gain primae facie evidence to instigate legal action where the legislation is complaint-based. Researchers are in a unique position because they are in receipt of employer responses to all applicants. The type of responses that have been obtained for a matched pair that indicate dishonest concealment of the reason for rejection have been reported by the ILO, McGinnity et al. (2009) and Riach and Rich (1991). These type of responses either tell the minority applicant they have been rejected because the job vacancy has been filled only to contact the majority applicant the following day to ask them to make a time for interview, or to tell the minority applicant they are over-qualified for the job at the same time inviting the equivalently qualified majority applicant to an interview. This raises the issue of the legislative framework of anti-discrimination laws and perhaps is an issue equal employment bodies and others could pursue more vigorously.

Recent tests in Australia, France and the USA have investigated the impact of different levels of qualification on callback (response) rates, investigating whether higher qualified applicants receive a higher positive response. Most of these tests have found that a higher qualification aided the majority applicant but not the minority applicant. The very first researchers to use written tests, Jowell and Prescott-Clarke (1970), were conscious of this issue. Of the total CVs they sent, half gave their immigrant applicant a higher qualification than the British white applicant and the other half gave the immigrant and British applicants equivalent qualifications. Jowell and Prescott-Clarke found no statistical significance in response rate to the higher qualified immigrant as compared to the British applicant, nevertheless the higher qualified immigrant did receive more positive responses. This has been echoed in research work that has been undertaken in Australia and France, where it was found that the higher qualification did not increase the response rate to the minority applicant but did increase the white applicant's chance of a callback.

Most of these studies conduct regression analysis with the callback rate as the dependent variable and, for the labour market tests, independent variables such as the ethnicity or sex of the recruiter, the percentage of immigrants in the workforce of the firm, the percentage of immigrants in the neighbourhood of the firm, the size of firm, whether the firm has an ethnic diversity or EEO policy, the proportion of the workforce that is male, whether it is public sector employment, job characteristics (such as the occupations), and résumé characteristics. Rarely were any of the independent variables found to be of statistical significance except those variables that the researchers had specifically controlled on the résumé, such as name, qualification or socioeconomic background.

Another addition to the experimental approach that could be considered is the Implicit Association Test (IAT) developed by psychologists. A detailed description of IAT procedures can be found in Al Ramiah et al. (this volume). Two recent studies conducted in Australia and Sweden have used the IAT to test employers' discriminatory attitudes. The researchers did not specifically test those employers that had been approached in their field experiments. If possible, it would be interesting to test those employers to which applications had been sent to investigate if there is any relation between discriminatory attitudes and the responses received.

Finally, a number of the studies have sent up to twelve applications for an advertised position. Firstly, there is importantly the ethical issue that testing takes up the time of employers and so sending many applications may impose more than trivial costs on employers. The other issue is contaminating the pool of job applicants: the researcher may send out twelve applications but they do not know how many other applications the employer receives. If it is, say, eight, the employer receives twenty in total, of which more than half are from the researcher. Further, it would be valuable for comparative purposes if tests sending multiple applications reported both callback rates and matched net discrimination levels as in the recent Irish study by McGinnity et al. (2009). So a cautionary note is sounded for the conduct of future experiments involving multiple applications for a specific vacancy.

References

Al Ramiah, A., Hewstone, M., Dovidio, J.F. and Penner, L.A. (2010) 'The Social Psychology of Discrimination: Theory, Measurement and Consequences' in L. Bond, F. McGinnity and H. Russell (eds.) *Making Equality Count: Irish and International Research Measuring Equality and Discrimination* Dublin: The Liffey Press.

Ayres, I. (1991). 'Fair driving: race and gender discrimination in retail car negotiations'. *Harvard Law Review*, Vol. 104, pp. 817-72.

Ayres, I. and Siegelman, P. (1995). 'Gender and race discrimination in bargaining for a new car'. *American Economic Review*, Vol. 85, pp. 304-21.

Daniel, W. (1968). *Racial Discrimination in England*. Middlesex: Penguin.

Ellemers, N. and Baretto, M. (2009). 'Collective action in modern times: How modern expressions of prejudice prevent collective action', *Journal of Social Issues*, Vol. 65, No. 4, pp. 749-768.

Jowell, R., and Prescott-Clarke, P. (1970). 'Racial discrimination and white-collar workers in Britain', *Race*, Vol. 11, No. 4, pp. 397-417.

McGinnity, F., Nelson, J. Lunn, P. and Quinn, E. (2009). *Discrimination in Recruitment: Evidence from a Field Experiment*. Dublin: Equality Authority and The Economic and Social Research Institute.

Riach, P.A. and Rich, J. (2004). 'Fishing for Discrimination', *Review of Social Economy*, Vol. 61, No. 4, pp. 465-486.

Riach, P.A. and Rich, J. (2002). 'Field experiments of discrimination in the market place', *Economic Journal*, Vol. 112, No. 483, pp. F480-F518.

Riach, P.A. and Rich, J. (1991). 'Testing for racial discrimination in the labour market', *Cambridge Journal of Economics*, Vol. 15, pp. 239-256.

Rich, J. and Judge, G. (2010). 'Measuring Discrimination: What do field experiments of markets tell us?' *Working Paper*, Department of Economics, University of Portsmouth. (contact author judy.rich@port.ac.uk)

Chapter 4

Are Eamon and Eithne More Employable than Hardeep and Heike? Evidence from a Field Experiment in Ireland

Frances McGinnity, Jacqueline Nelson,
Peter D. Lunn and Emma Quinn

In recent years there has been significant immigration into Ireland of non-Irish nationals in a context of rapid economic and employment growth. In the 1996 Census just under 2 per cent of the population was born outside Ireland and the UK; by the 2006 Census this figure was over 8 per cent.[1] This has given rise to concerns about discrimination in the Irish labour market. While it is clear that discrimination is damaging both for individuals and Irish society as a whole, it is very difficult to measure, and there is little direct evidence about the extent and nature of discrimination in Ireland. Breaking new ground in Irish research, this chapter describes a study which provides direct evidence of discrimination using a field experiment on discrimination in recruitment on the basis of nationality/ethnicity in the Irish labour market.

The idea of our experiment is simple: two individuals who are identical on all relevant characteristics other than the poten-

---

[1] Nationality and ethnicity questions were not asked in the 1996 census so place of birth is the most useful indicator for comparison.

tial basis of discrimination apply for the same jobs. Responses are carefully recorded, and discrimination or the lack thereof is then measured as the extent to which one applicant is invited to interview relative to the other applicant.

Why an experiment? While much recent immigration to Ireland has been driven by labour market demand, there is a growing body of evidence pointing to the labour market disadvantage of immigrants in Ireland. For example, compared to Irish nationals, this group experiences higher levels of unemployment (O'Connell and McGinnity, 2008), suffers a wage penalty (Barrett and McCarthy, 2007) and is much more likely to report work-related discrimination (Russell et al., this volume). However, as discussed in the introduction to this volume, comparing labour market outcomes and self-reports of discrimination give only indirect indications of discrimination (Darity and Mason, 1998). The major advantage of field experiments is that they provide direct observations of unequal treatment.

In fact, controlled field experiments of this nature are a well-established approach to testing directly for discrimination (e.g. Bertrand and Mullainathan, 2004; Petit, 2007; Carlsson and Rooth, 2007; Rich, this volume – see Riach and Rich, 2002 and Bassanini and Saint-Martin, 2008 for reviews), though not in Ireland prior to this study. In almost all cases of tests for racial discrimination a White applicant is matched to a non-White applicant, but in many studies, White immigrants are also included to distinguish 'race' from 'foreignness' or immigrant status. The national/ethnic background of a candidate is almost always signalled by the applicant's name, as in this experiment (Riach and Rich, 2002).

What is remarkable is the consistency of recorded discrimination in previous studies. This is in spite of cross-national differences in recruitment policies and large differences in the ethnic composition of the minority groups and their status in the host society. Indeed field experiments have found widespread evidence of discrimination in recruitment: against Indians, Pakistanis, West Indians and Africans in Britain; against African-Americans and Hispanics in the US; against Vietnamese in Australia; against Asians in Sweden and North Africans in France (Riach and Rich, 2002; Bertrand and Mullainathan, 2004; Carlsson and Rooth, 2007; Cediey and Foroni, 2008).

A second consistent finding is that of lower discrimination against White immigrants in predominantly White societies, in the studies which tested this (e.g. Jowell and Prescott-Clarke, 1970; Firth, 1981; Riach and Rich, 1991).

The findings on variations across the labour market are far less consistent. Indeed, many field experiments do not test variation across the labour market at all. Of those that have done so, while some studies found no difference between skill levels (Bertrand and Mullainathan, 2004), others recorded higher discrimination among low-skilled jobs (Carlsson and Rooth, 2007). Some experiments recorded higher discrimination among smaller firms (Carlsson and Rooth, 2007), yet others did not (Bertrand and Mullainathan, 2004).

Given that this is the first time this research has been conducted in Ireland and that there is a recent history of migration, we test for the presence of discrimination against a number of groups. Following checks for the plausibility of the minority groups using census data, those selected were: Asian, African and German. This chapter addresses the following research questions:

- Firstly, are there any differences in responses to the minority candidates and the Irish candidate? Given both previous international findings from field experiments and the differential outcomes identified in the Irish labour market, we expect that we will find some discrimination against minority candidates. As this is the first field experiment in Ireland, we have no prior assumptions about the extent of this discrimination, which varies substantially across countries.

- Secondly, is there any variation in the extent of discrimination between the minority groups? Previous field experiments from other countries would suggest higher discrimination in recruitment against non-White immigrants than White immigrants. Thus we might expect higher discrimination in recruitment against African applicants, followed by Asian applicants, followed by European (German) job applicants.

- Thirdly, does discrimination vary across the labour market in Ireland? As noted above, because of the nature of the field experiment method, we are limited as to how much variation we can test. What we can examine is whether discrimination varies by occupation, industrial sector and by time period.

We adapted the standard methodology for the Irish case, and in the next section we present the design of the experiment. We then present the results of the experiment, outlining the extent of discrimination against non-Irish nationals in recruitment in Ireland. In the conclusion we summarise the results, and reflect on possible explanations and the policy implications of our findings. This chapter presents a short summary of the study. For further details of the research design and the findings, the reader should consult the project report, McGinnity et al., 2009.

Experimental Design

Key Design Features

In designing the experiment, we followed international best practice, adapting it to the Irish situation. Reviewing field experiments, Heckman and Siegelman (1993) criticise personal approaches, i.e. the use of matched pairs of testers who pose as job applicants in real job searches, for not being able to demonstrate the equivalence of tester. Written applications, or correspondence tests, have the advantage that they allow maximum control and a guarantee of equivalence, and this is the approach taken in this study. Correspondence testing does have a number of limitations. Probably the most salient weakness is that using this method, only a limited number of jobs are available for testing, namely those requiring a written application. Correspondence tests are also confined to the first stage of the hiring process, i.e. selection to interview. However, this need not be a serious problem, as evidence from the ILO studies suggests that most discrimination occurs at the initial stage (i.e. selection for interview), not at the stage 'interview to job offer' (Bovenkerk, 1992).

Operational decisions were guided by a number of general considerations. Firstly, we wished to avoid detection in a small labour market. Thus we only ever sent out two CVs, not up to six, as in other countries (e.g. Petit, 2007) to avoid arousing suspicion. CVs were designed to be equivalent but not identical. Work experience was with fictitious employers. Third-level degrees were from existing universities but non-existent courses. Secondly, there were ethical considerations. We wanted to minimise inconvenience, costs and damage to the reputation of employers, who did not know they were part of an experiment.[2] Each employer was only sent one application, and interview offers were declined as quickly as possible, usually within 24 hours. Records were kept highly confidential. Thirdly, we faced constraints of time and financial resources. This was a funded project with dedicated funds and deadlines. Occupations with many vacancies were required to reduce the time required to conduct the experiment. After monitoring the rate of vacancies in different occupations, three occupations were finally selected for investigation: lower administration, lower accountancy and retail sales positions Finally, we wanted to create high-quality

---

[2] Experiments such as this raise a number of ethical issues, discussed in detail in Riach and Rich, 2004. This project went through a rigorous ethics procedure before it commenced (see McGinnity et al., 2009).

CVs that were realistic and plausible for the jobs advertised. The higher the rate of response to CVs, the fewer CVs need to be sent out. Thus male names were used for the financial CVs, female names for the lower administrative and sales' CVs. Previous research has shown that women are much more likely to be called to interview for administrative jobs than men (Riach and Rich, 2002).

Development of Fictitious Applicants' CVs

For each occupation, two equivalent CVs were developed.[3] In order to avoid detection, CVs were not identical, but within each job category all relevant personal and employment characteristics other than national or ethnic origin were matched between the two CVs. Essentially, applicants differed only in their ethnically distinctive names. The effectiveness of this field experiment depended on employers recognising the ethnicity of job applicants. A shortlist of potential names was developed based on registers of ethnically common names and web searches. A small pre-test was then conducted to identify names which were most readily identifiable as Irish, African, Asian or European (German). Hardeep, Heike, Eamon and Eithne are examples of the types of names used.

The brief CVs developed for this study included the following information: personal and contact details, education, work experience, hobbies/interests and other skills. Fictitious candidates were all young, in order to be as plausible as possible. The recent nature of migration into Ireland means that most minority job applicants would not have been in the country long enough to have been at school in Ireland. However, all our fictitious candidates had an Irish Leaving Certificate, thus indicating English-language proficiency. It was decided that equivalence of

---

[3] For illustrative CVs, see McGinnity et al., 2009.

CVs and, in particular, English language fluency, was more important than whether these candidates were 'typical' of their group currently living in Ireland. Irish nationality was typically indicated on minority CVs to indicate to employers that there were no potential issues concerning work permits, right to work in Ireland etc.

Applying for Jobs

The approach used was to respond to advertised vacancies so the first stage in the application procedure was to identify vacancies in each of the three target areas: lower administration, lower accountancy and retail sales. A number of different sources were used in the job search, including both online and newspaper job advertisements.

Once a suitable vacancy had been identified, two matched CVs were sent by email to the advertising employer. To minimise the likelihood of detection the two CVs were sent a few hours apart. The CVs were also rotated across identities. When CV1 was sent, it was identical across the four different ethnic identities; the only variations were the names and email addresses of the applicants. The same applied for CV2. There were no significant differences in type of response to CV1 and CV2 in any of the three occupations.[4] The first applications were sent out in early March 2008 and the final applications at the end of September 2008.

Voicemail and email addresses were typically checked for responses once every working day. Of the 240 job advertisements responded to, responses were received in respect of 111 of them in total (including rejections). Both telephone and email responses were recorded, and response rates were similar across occupations and minority groups. Approximately 39 per cent of jobs ap-

---

[4] Administration: $\chi^2(2)=0.141$, p=0.932; accountancy: $\chi^2(2)=0.287$, p=0.866; retail sales: $\chi^2(2)=0.054$, p=0.973.

plied for received at least one favourable response; this relatively high rate of positive responses is indicative of the quality of the CVs.[5] All responses were recorded electronically and hard copy records were also kept on a confidential basis. Once an employer responded to an application, the research team needed to decline any offers made as promptly as possible, usually within 24 hours, in order to minimise inconvenience to employers.

Results: Discrimination in Recruitment

Scale of Discrimination

What were the responses to our matched pairs of fictional applicants? Table 1 presents a breakdown of outcomes relating to the 240 pairs of matched job applications. Of these, no response was received or both candidates were rejected in 147 cases. The remaining 93 cases are classified into three categories: those where both candidates were invited to interview, those where the candidate with the 'Irish' name was asked to interview and the candidate with the 'minority' name was not, and those where the minority candidate was invited to interview but the Irish candidate was not.

Our first research question was whether there are any differences in responses to the minority candidates and the Irish candidate. As is clear from Table 1, the incidence of an interview being granted to the Irish candidate but not the minority candidate is substantially higher than the incidence of an interview being granted to the minority candidate but not the Irish candidate. If we refer to these cases of non-equal treatment as 'discrimination', then discrimination against each of the three minorities is greater than discrimination against the Irish candidates. We provide an explicit comparison between the three mi-

---

[5] This includes jobs where either both candidates were invited to interview, or just one candidate (93 out of 240 jobs).

norities regarding the scale of discrimination in the next section. Concentrating for now on the total figures in the final column of Table 1, discrimination against the non-Irish candidate occurred in 55 cases, while discrimination against the Irish candidate occurred in just 15 cases.

Table 1: Classification of Outcomes to Matched Job Applications by Minority

	Irish/ African	Irish/ Asian	Irish/ German	Total
No response/ both rejected	54	46	47	147
Both invited	4	8	11	23
Irish invited, minority not	18	19	18	55
Minority invited, Irish not	5	7	3	15
Net discrimination (Row 3- Row 4)	13	12	15	40
Discrimination rate (Row 3 – Row 4)/(Row 2+ Row 3 + Row 4)	48%	35%	47%	43%
Relative callback rate (Irish/Minority)	2.44	1.80	2.07	2.05

Some discrimination against majority White applicants is typically found in experiments of this nature, and is usually ascribed to a randomness/inefficiency in the recruitment process (Riach and Rich, 2002). This is why all estimates of discrimination we discuss below are of net discrimination (see row 5), i.e. discrimination against the minority minus discrimination against the Irish candidate. In this case net discrimination for the total sample is 40.

One standard measure of the extent of discrimination is the 'discrimination rate', which measures the difference between discrimination in favour of the Irish candidate and discrimination in favour of the non-Irish candidate, or 'net discrimination', as a proportion of those instances where at least one candidate was invited to interview. Discrimination rates are provided in the penultimate row (row 6) of Table 1.

Although commonly employed in studies such as this, the discrimination rate is not unproblematic as a measure of discrimination. The difficulty is that it is not clear which denominator is the most appropriate for comparison. That is, should we measure net discrimination as a percentage of all applications sent, of applications for which responses were received, or of applications for which at least one candidate was invited to interview? In Table 1, we have conformed to practice elsewhere and used the latter, but there is debate about this in the literature (Heckman and Siegelman, 1993; Riach and Rich, 2002).

Instead, we prefer to highlight the 'relative callback rate' of being asked to interview, which is provided in the final row of Table 1. This is defined as the odds that the Irish candidate is asked to interview relative to the odds that the minority candidate is invited. More simply, it tells us how much more likely it is that the Irish candidate is asked to interview. The advantage of using the relative callback rate is that it is independent of the denominator.

In the present case, from the final column of Table 1 we can see that Irish candidates are invited to interview a total of 78 times (counting total column, rows 2 and 3), while minority candidates are invited a total of 38 times (total column, rows 2 and 4). For a given denominator N, the relative callback rate is:

$$\frac{78/N}{38/N} = \frac{78}{38} = 2.05$$

That is, in our experiment candidates with an Irish name are over twice as likely to be asked to attend an interview as are candidates with an African, Asian or German name. This is the scale of discrimination encountered.

An alternative way of expressing this considers how many applications candidates need to send out to get a positive response. From Table 1 we see that, of 240 applications (total column of rows 1 to 4), Irish candidates received 78 positive responses in total, minority candidates received 38 positive responses. Thus, on average, Irish candidates had to respond to 3.08 (240/78) vacancies to receive one positive response, whereas minority applicants had to respond to 6.32 (240/38) vacancies to receive one positive response, both using identical CVs.

The answer to our first research question then is clearly yes: there are clear differences between Irish and minority candidates in their chances of being called to interview.

What form did this differential treatment take? These are some examples of actual responses received, to illustrate the results presented in Table 1.

> A Receptionist/Administrator position is advertised and the African and Irish candidates respond to the advertisement. The Irish candidate is told that the position she applied for has since been filled, but that the company has two other positions that may be suitable. The African applicant receives no response.

> The day after an Irish and an Asian candidate applied for a Coordinator/Administrator position, the Irish candidate was asked to call back regarding her CV. The Asian candidate received an email at the same time stating: 'I regret to inform you the position is now filled.'

Is this Discrimination Statistically Significant?

Although at first sight this disparity is striking, are the differences in treatment between Irish and minority candidates statistically significant?

For a given level of positive responses to candidates' applications, the appropriate comparison is between those cases where the Irish candidate is invited and the minority candidate is not and those where the minority candidate is invited and the Irish candidate is not. When we apply a statistical test using a binomial distribution, the result is a p-value that equates to the probability that the data could have been observed if, in reality, there were no greater likelihood of discrimination against the minority candidate than of discrimination against the Irish candidate.[6] The analysis can be done with the three different minorities pooled into a single group, or separately for each minority. The resulting p-values are given in Table 2.

Table 2: Statistical Significance Test for Higher Incidence of Discrimination against Minority Candidates than Irish Candidates

Minority	African	Asian	German	All
Discrimination rate	48%	35%	47%	43%
Relative call-back rate	2.44	1.80	2.07	2.05
p-value	0.005	0.014	0.001	0.000001

From the figures in Table 2 we can conclude that the higher incidence of discrimination affecting minority candidates is strongly statistically significant. Indeed, the tiny probability in the final column reveals that the chance of observing the outcomes in Table 1, if there were in fact no discrimination in the real world, is less than one in a million. According to conventional criteria for statistical significance, the level of discrimination against each of the three different minorities, considered separately, is also statistically significant.

---

[6] For further details of this test see McGinnity et al., 2009.

It is possible that the results thus far might be specific to a particular type of occupation; that minority candidates are discriminated against when applying for some types of jobs but not others. To examine this, Table 3 provides relative callback rates and p-values arising from similar significance tests with respect to each of the three occupations involved in the experiment.

Table 3: Relative Callback Rates and Significance Tests for Discrimination against Minority Candidates by Occupation

Occupation	Number of Cases Producing at Least One Invitation	Relative Callback Rate	p-value
Lower administration	56	2.04	0.001
Lower accountancy	20	2.00	0.038
Retail sales	17	2.17	0.059

The similarity in the estimated callback rates reveals a consistent level of discrimination across each of the three occupations. Candidates with Irish names are over twice as likely to be invited to interview for all three occupations. Meanwhile, the p-values in the final column confirm that this discrimination is statistically significant, albeit marginally so in the case of sales assistants, where the sample-size is smallest. Thus, the discrimination observed is not confined to a particular type of job, but applies across the three occupations involved in the experiment. When we test these findings using a variety of multivariate models we find no evidence of difference in discrimination rates by minority group, occupation, broad sector or time period within the experiment (see McGinnity et al., 2009 for further model estimates).[7]

How does the discrimination rate compare with similar international studies testing discrimination against minorities? As noted above, the callback rate observed in our study was just over 2, the discrimination rate 43 per cent. Callback rates vary considerably across studies, but in general rates are between 1 and 1.5, so the findings in Ireland are on the high side, though not the highest.[8]

Conclusion

Summary of the Findings of this Experiment

The findings of this experiment are easy to summarise. Firstly, candidates with Irish names are over twice as likely to be invited to interview for advertised jobs as candidates with identifiably non-Irish names. The chance of observing this outcome, if there were in fact no discrimination in the real world, is less than one in a million. An Eamon would be much more likely to be called to interview than a Hardeep, and an Eithne much more likely than a Heike, even if both were to submit equivalent CVs. Secondly, we find no differences in the degree of discrimination faced by candidates with Asian, African or German names. We might have detected differences between the groups with a larger number of cases, but in our sample all three are around half as likely to be invited to interview as Irish candidates. Thirdly, this finding is robust across occupations applied for and industrial sectors tested. The results indicate that there is strong discrimination

---

[7] Sectors were: non-market services; industry; transport/communication; other business and market services. Time periods were: March to mid-June; mid-June to mid-August; mid-August to end of September 2008.

[8] For example, the discrimination rate observed against Africans in France was 54 per cent (Cediey and Foroni, 2008). See McGinnity et al., 2009, Table 4.5 for further details.

against non-Irish candidates and this applies broadly across different jobs and sectors of the Irish labour market. The strength of the discrimination recorded in the present experiment is high relative to similar studies carried out in other countries.

Note that this experiment just tested the first stage of the recruitment process, invitation to interview. Once the entire process of hiring has been followed through with matched applicants, including attendance at interview, the likelihood is that discrimination faced would be even higher (Bovenkerk, 1992).

As with all experiments of this nature, a limited number of occupations were tested: lower administration, lower accountancy and retail sales. It is possible that a different discrimination rate would be found for recruitment in Ireland in either different occupations altogether, or higher-skilled positions in these occupations. The discrimination may also have varied had we tested different minorities. An experiment with a larger sample size might have detected some differences not observed with this sample, though we judge this to be unlikely.

Interpreting the Results

So why is discrimination in this stage of recruitment relatively high in Ireland, given the recent history of migration? We might have expected, given relatively positive attitudes to migrants (Hughes et al., 2007), that discrimination in recruitment would be lower than in countries with established minority groups. Secondly, why did we not observe significant variation between minority groups, as found in most other countries? There are a number of possible explanations.

In terms of theoretical perspectives, two broad groups of economic theories dominate the literature: taste based and statistical discrimination models.[9] For statistical discrimination mod-

---

[9] See Darity and Mason (1998) for a comprehensive review of these, and other, models of discrimination.

els, imperfect information about workers' abilities constitutes the key rationale for discrimination to arise. In one class of statistical discrimination models, potential employers cannot observe everything they wish to know about job candidates, and in this environment, they have an incentive to use group membership as a signal that allows them to improve their predictions of a candidate's ability to perform (e.g. Phelps, 1972; Arrow, 1973). Employers assume that individual characteristics, like ethnicity, are correlated with the unobserved determinants of performance. Individuals are assigned the expected abilities of the groups they belong to. These models would suggest that Irish employers assess minority candidates as having lower productivity, linked to language skills, knowledge of local labour markets etc and therefore would not be able to do the job as well.

However, the candidates in this experiment had identical qualifications and work experience, all of which were obtained in Ireland. Thus, the CVs strongly indicated good English language skills, and employers did not have to form judgements based on foreign degrees or work experience, or even secondary schooling. That said, we cannot rule out the possibility that employers use minority status as a proxy for unobserved productivity differences, such as character and motivation.

These findings certainly suggest that employers may not appreciate the equivalence of CVs. Employers receiving many CVs might use quick heuristics (as in 'a rule of thumb that can backfire') when reading them. One such heuristic may be that they read no further when they see a minority name. If employers did not read past the name on the CV, they may have assumed that the minority candidates would not have the requisite language skills for the positions applied for; would have less experience of working in Ireland or some other (inaccurate) pre-conception of the CV that followed.

The prominent alternative to statistical discrimination – taste-based discrimination models – sees discrimination as based on prejudice (Becker, 1971).[10] The basic idea is that prejudiced employers will prefer majority applicants and impose a penalty for minority applicants, which lowers the wages and employment rates of minority workers (Bassanini and Saint-Martin, 2008). If this is due to ethnic or racial prejudice, we should expect higher discrimination in recruitment against ethnic minority applicants – African and Asian applicants – than against the German applicant, and yet this is not what we found. Alternatively, if this prejudice takes the form of 'xenophobia' (i.e. fear of foreigners), the penalty would be the same for all non-Irish groups. This explanation is just not consistent with previous research on attitudes to migrants in Ireland, which are generally positive (Hughes et al., 2007).

Rather than feelings as hostile as xenophobia, the finding of no difference in assessments of minority groups may be more a question of 'in-group favouritism'. In-group favouritism implies the extension of trust, positive regard, cooperation and empathy to in-group, but not out-group, members, and while it is an initial form of discrimination, it does not entail an active component of aggression, as in out-group derogation (Hewstone et al., 2002). In our case, in-group favouritism would translate into the positive desire to hire Irish workers, as opposed to a dislike of hiring foreign workers. It is consistent with the Irish situation of an existing strong, cohesive national identity, based on an almost exclusively White Irish population, and until very recently, no substantial non-Irish minority groups to either threaten or be included as part of that identity.

We cannot fully rule out alternatives, like statistical discrimination or xenophobia, but we feel that the unequal treatment we observe in this experiment is most consistent with (1) a

---

[10] In the following we limit the discussion to employer prejudice. See Darity and Mason (1998) or Bassanini and Saint-Martin (2008) for a discussion of customer or co-worker prejudice.

strong preference for Irish candidates on the part of these employers/recruiters (in-group favouritism) and/or (2) a failure by employers to appreciate that the candidates' CVs were equivalent, because of not reading past the name on the CV. Nevertheless, whatever is driving the discrimination it makes it no less serious a problem.

Policy Implications

In terms of policy, Ireland has relatively robust legislation prohibiting discrimination in recruitment on the basis of ethnic or national origin, as well as a range of other grounds. Yet it is clear from this experiment that discrimination in recruitment against minority groups in Ireland is relatively high. As noted by the OECD (2008) legal prohibition of discrimination can only be effective if it is enforced, and in most OECD countries enforcement relies on victims' willingness to assert their claims. Yet many individuals are not even aware of their rights, or aware that they have been discriminated against. Our findings underline the need for dedicating resources to the promotion of equality.

There are a number of possible measures that may help reduce such discrimination and promote good equality practice in recruitment. Firstly, the dissemination of information from the international literature on the benefits of diversity. Secondly, more information for both employers and job seekers about what the equality legislation permits and prohibits. Thirdly, developing guidelines for all employers to ensure their recruitment practices are not likely to be discriminatory. A fourth possibility is the introduction of random audits of hiring practices – analogous to financial audits. If employers were required to keep all records of job applications for a period and obliged –in the event of a random audit – to justify decisions on short-listing for interview and final choice of candidate, it would reinforce the pressure for good practice in the hiring decision.

What is clear from this experiment is that the extent of employer discrimination in recruitment observed is such that equality in recruitment will not be achieved until discrimination is tackled effectively.

References

Arrow, K. (1973) 'The theory of discrimination' in Ashenfelter, P. and Rees, A. (eds.) *Discrimination in Labor Markets*. Princeton, NJ: Princeton University Press.

Barrett, A. and McCarthy, Y. (2007); 'Immigrants in a Booming Economy: Analysing their Earnings and Welfare Dependence', *Labour*, Vol. 21, No. 4.

Bassanini, A. and Saint-Martin, A. (2008) 'The Price of Prejudice: Labour market discriminatin on the grounds of gender and ethnicity'. Chapter 3 in *Employment Outlook*. Paris: OECD.

Becker, G. (1971) *The Economics of Discrimination*. Second Edition. Chicago: University of Chicago Press.

Bertrand, M. and Mullainathan, S. (2004) 'Are Emily and Greg More Employable than Lakisha and Jamal? A Field Experiment on Labor Market Discrimination', *The American Economic Review*, Vol. 94, No. 4, pp. 991-1013.

Bovenkerk, F. (1992) *Testing Discrimination in Natural Experiments. A Manual for international comparative research on discrimination on the grounds of 'race' and ethnic origin*. Geneva: ILO.

Carlsson, M. and Rooth, D.-O. (2007) 'Evidence of ethnic discrimination in the Swedish labor market using experimental data', in *Labour Economics*, Vol. 14: 716-729.

Cediey, E. and Foroni, F. (2008) 'Discrimination in access to employment on grounds of foreign origin in France', ILO International Migration Paper No. 85E. Geneva: ILO.

Darity, W. and Mason, P. (1998) 'Evidence on discrimination in employment: codes of color, codes of gender', *Journal of Economic Perspectives*, Vol. 12, pp. 63-90.

Firth, M. (1981) 'Racial Discrimination in the British Labor Market', *Industrial and Labor Relations Review*, Vol. 34, No. 2, pp. 265-272.

Heckman, J. and Siegelman, P. (1993) 'The Urban Institute audit studies: Their methods and findings'. In M. Fix and R. Struyk, *Clear and Convinc-*

ing Evidence: Measurement of Discrimination in America. Washington DC: The Urban Institute Press.

Hewstone, M., Rubin, R. and Willis, H. (2002) 'Intergroup bias' *Annual Review of Psychology* 53: 575-60.

Hughes, G. McGinnity, F. O'Connell, P. and Quinn, E. (2007) 'The Impact of Migration' in T. Fahey, H. Russell and C. Whelan, *Best of Times? The Social Impact of the Celtic Tiger*. Dublin: IPA.

Jowell, R. and Prescott-Clarke, P. (1970) 'Racial Discrimination and White-collar Workers in Britain', *Race*, Vol. 11, No. 4.

McGinnity, F., Nelson, J., Lunn, P. and Quinn, E. (2009) *Discrimination in Recruitment: Evidence from a field experiment*. Dublin: The Equality Authority and The Economic and Social Research Institute.

O'Connell, P.J. and McGinnity, F. (2008) *Immigrants at Work: Nationality and Ethnicity in the Irish Labour Market*. Dublin: The Equality Authority and The Economic and Social Research Institute.

OECD (2008) *Ending Job Discrimination*. OECD Policy Brief, July 2008. Paris: OECD.

Petit, P. (2007) 'The effects of age and family constraints on gender hiring discrimination: A field experiment in the French financial sector', *Labour Economics*, Vol. 14, Issue 3, pp. 371-391.

Phelps, E. (1972) 'The Statistical Theory of Racism and Sexism'. *American Economic Review*, September, 62 (4).

Riach, P. and Rich, J. (1991) 'Testing for racial discrimination in the labour market', *Cambridge Journal of Economics*, Vol. 15, pp. 239-56.

Riach, P. and Rich, J. (2002) 'Field experiments of discrimination in the market place' in *The Economic Journal*, 112, F480-F518.

Riach, P. and Rich, J. (2004) 'Deceptive field experiments of discrimination: Are they ethical?' *Kyklos* 57 (3), pp. 457-470.

Rich, J. (2010) 'Measuring Discrimination: What do Field Experiments of Markets Tell Us' in L. Bond, F. McGinnity and H. Russell (eds.) *Making Equality Count: Irish and International Research Measuring Equality and Discrimination* Dublin: The Liffey Press.

Russell, H., McGinnity, F., Quinn, E. and King, O'Riain (2010) 'The Experience of Discrimination in Ireland: Evidence from Self-Report Data' in L. Bond, F. McGinnity and H. Russell (eds.) *Making Equality Count: Irish and International Research Measuring Equality and Discrimination* Dublin: The Liffey Press.

Chapter 5

The Social Psychology of Discrimination: Theory, Measurement and Consequences

Ananthi Al Ramiah, Miles Hewstone,
John F. Dovidio and Louis A. Penner

Social psychologists engage with the prevalence and problems of discrimination by studying the processes that underlie it. Understanding when discrimination is likely to occur suggests ways that we can overcome it. In this chapter, we begin by discussing the ways in which social psychologists talk about discrimination and discuss its prevalence. Second, we outline some theories underlying the phenomenon. Third, we consider the ways in which social psychological studies have measured discrimination, discussing findings from laboratory and field studies with explicit and implicit measures. Fourth, we consider the systemic consequences of discrimination and their implications for intergroup relations, social mobility and personal wellbeing. Finally, we provide a summary and some conclusions.

Defining Discrimination

Social psychologists are careful to disentangle discrimination from its close cousins of prejudice and stereotypes. Prejudice refers to an unjustifiable negative attitude toward a group and its individual members. Stereotypes are beliefs about the personal attributes of a group of people, and can be over-generalised, inaccurate, and resistant to change in the presence of new information. Discrimination refers to unjustifiable negative behaviour towards a group or its members, where behaviour is adjudged to include both actions towards, and judgements/decisions about, group members. Correll et al. (2010, p. 46) provide a very useful definition of discrimination as 'behaviour directed towards category members that is consequential for their outcomes and that is directed towards them not because of any particular deservingness or reciprocity, but simply because they happen to be members of that category'. The notion of 'deservingness' is central to the expression and experience of discrimination. It is not an objectively defined criterion but one that has its roots in historical and present-day inequalities and societal norms. Perpetrators may see their behaviours as justified by the deservingness of the targets, while the targets themselves may disagree. Thus the behaviours, which some judge to be discriminatory, will not be seen as such by others.

The expression of discrimination can broadly be classified into two types: overt or direct, and subtle, unconscious or automatic. Manifestations include verbal and non-verbal hostility (Darley and Fazio, 1980; Word et al., 1974), avoidance of contact (Cuddy et al., 2007; Pettigrew and Tropp, 2006), aggressive approach behaviours (Cuddy, et al., 2007) and the denial of opportunities and access or equal treatment (Bobo, 2001; Sidanius and Pratto, 1999).

Across a range of domains, cultures and historical periods, there are and have been systemic disparities between members of dominant and non-dominant groups (Sidaniuis and Pratto, 1999). For example, ethnic minorities consistently experience worse health outcomes (Barnett and Halverson, 2001; Underwood et al., 2004), worse school performance (Cohen et al., 2006), and harsher treatment in the justice system (Steffensmeier and Demuth, 2000). In both business and academic domains, women are paid less and hold positions of lower status than men, controlling for occupation and qualifications (Goldman et al., 2006). In terms of the labour market, sociological research shows that ethnic minority applicants tend to suffer from a phenomenon known as the ethnic penalty. Ethnic penalties are defined as the net disadvantages experienced by ethnic minorities after controlling for their educational qualifications, age and experience in the labour market (Heath and McMahon, 1997). While the ethnic penalty cannot be equated with discrimination, discrimination is likely to be a major factor responsible for its existence. This discrimination ranges from unequal treatment that minority group members receive during the application process, and over the course of their education and socialisation, which can have grave consequences for the existence of 'bridging' social networks, 'spatial mismatch' between labour availability and opportunity, and differences in aspirations and preferences (Heath and McMahon, 1997).

Theories of Discrimination

Several theories have shaped our understanding of intergroup relations, prejudice and discrimination, and we focus on four here: the social identity perspective, the 'behaviours from intergroup affect and stereotypes' map, aversive racism theory and system justification theory.

As individuals living in a social context, we traverse the continuum between our personal and collective selves. Different social contexts lead to the salience of particular group memberships (Turner et al., 1987). The first theoretical framework that we outline, the social identity perspective (Tajfel and Turner, 1979) holds that group members are motivated to protect their self-esteem and achieve a positive and distinct social identity. This drive for a positive social identity can result in discrimination, which is expressed as either direct harm to the outgroup, or more commonly and spontaneously, as giving preferential treatment to the ingroup, a phenomenon known as ingroup bias.

Going further, and illustrating the general tendency that humans have to discriminate, the minimal group paradigm studies (Tajfel and Turner, 1986) reveal how mere categorisation as a group member can lead to ingroup bias, the favouring of ingroup members over outgroup members in evaluations and allocation of resources (Turner, 1978). In the minimal group paradigm studies, participants are classified as belonging to arbitrary groups (e.g. people who tend to overestimate or underestimate the number of dots presented to them) and evaluate members of the ingroup and outgroup, and take part in a reward allocation task (Tajfel and Turner, 1986) between the two groups. Results across hundreds of studies show that participants rate ingroup members more positively, exhibit preference for ingroup members in allocation of resources, and want to maintain maximal difference in allocation between ingroup and outgroup members, thereby giving outgroup members less than an equality norm would require. Given the fact that group membership in this paradigm does not involve a deeply-held attachment and operates within the wider context of equality norms, this tendency to discriminate is an important finding, and indicative of the spontaneous nature of prejudice and discrimination in intergroup contexts (Al Ramiah et al., in press). Whereas social categorisation is sufficient to create discriminatory treatment, often motivated by ingroup favouritism, direct competition between groups exacerbates this bias, typically generating responses directly to disadvantage the outgroup, as well (Sherif et al., 1961).

Whereas social identity theory examines basic, general processes leading to intergroup discrimination, the BIAS map (Behaviours from Intergroup Affect and Stereotypes; see Cuddy, et al., 2007) offers insights into the specific ways that we discriminate against members of particular types of groups. The BIAS map (Figure 1) is an extension of the Stereotype Content Model (Fiske et al., 2002), and proposes that the relative status and competitiveness of groups determine the stereotype content of warmth and competence attributed to the outgroup.

Figure 1: The BIAS Map: Behaviours from Intergroup Affect and Stereotypes (Cuddy et al., 2007)

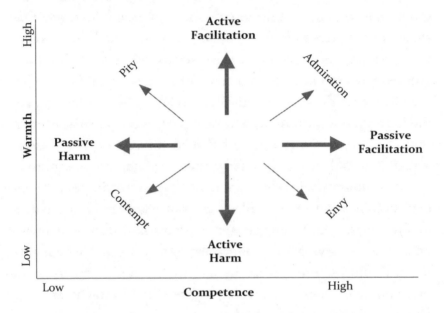

These stereotypes predict affect towards the outgroup, and affect predicts action tendencies. Group stereotypes contain a mixture of competence and warmth attributes, and this combination of content gives rise to particular emotions and action tendencies. The warmth dimension of stereotypes, which carries greater weight in social encounters (Cuddy et al., 2007; Van Lange and Kuhlman, 1994; Vonk, 1999; Wojciszke et al., 1998), predicts active behavioural tendencies while the secondary dimension of competence predicts more passive tendencies. Negative active and passive behaviours can be construed by targets as constituting discrimination, and can have significant impact on the quality of their lives. Examples of negative passive behaviours are ignoring another's presence, not making eye contact with them, excluding members of certain groups from getting opportunities, and so on, while examples of negative active behaviours include supporting institutional racism or voting for anti-immigration political parties. These examples show that discriminatory behaviours can range from the subtle to the overt, and the particular views that we have about each outgroup determines the manifestation of discrimination.

The third theory that we consider, aversive racism (Dovidio and Gaertner, 2004) complements social identity theory (which suggests the pervasiveness of intergroup discrimination) and the BIAS map (which helps identify the form in which discrimination will be manifested) by further identifying when discrimination will be manifested or inhibited. The aversive racism framework essentially evolved to understand the psychological conflict that afflicts many White Americans with regard to their racial attitudes. Changing social norms increasingly prohibit prejudice and discrimination towards minority and other stigmatised groups (Crandall et al., 2002), and work in the United States has shown that appearing racist has become aversive to many White Americans (Dovidio and Gaertner, 2004; Gaertner and Dovidio, 1986; Katz and Hass, 1988; McConahay, 1986) in terms not only of their public image but also of their private self concept. However, a multitude of individual and societal factors continue to reinforce stereotypes and negative evaluative biases (which are rooted, in part, in biases identified by social identity theory), which result in continued expression and experience of discrimination. Equality norms give rise to considerable psychological conflict in which people regard prejudice as unjust and offensive, but remain unable to fully suppress their own biases. Thus ethnic and racial attitudes have become more complex than they were in the past.

According to the aversive racism framework, people resolve this conflict by upholding egalitarian norms and simultaneously maintaining subtle or automatic forms of prejudice. Specifically, people generally will not discriminate in situations in which right and wrong is clearly defined; discrimination would be obvious to others and to oneself, and aversive racists do not want to appear or be discriminatory. However, aversive racists will systematically discriminate when appropriate behaviours are not clearly prescribed or they can justify their behaviour on the basis of some factor other than race (see Dovidio and Gaertner, 2004).

The pervasiveness of discrimination and its systematic, and often subtle, expression shapes society in ways that perpetuate inequities. The final theory that we outline is system justification theory, which hinges on the finding that low-status groups in 'unequal social systems ... internalize a sense of personal or collective inferiority' (Jost et al., 2001, p. 367). System justification theorists argue that the social identity perspective posited need for positive distinctiveness as a function of feeling good about oneself (ego justification) and one's group (group justification) is related (positively or negatively, depending on your status) to the belief that the system in which the groups are based is fair (Jost and Banaji, 1994). For high-status groups, ego and group justification correspond to a belief that the system is just and that their high-status is a reward for their worthiness. This leads to ingroup bias. People with a history of personal and group advantage often derive the prescriptive from the descriptive, or in other words, labour under the 'is-ought' illusion (Hume, 1939); they believe that as this is what the world looks like and has looked like for a long time, this is in fact what it *should* look like. For low-status group members, however, these justification needs can be at odds (Jost and Burgess, 2000) if they believe that the system is just. Their low-status can be seen as deserved punishment for their unworthiness and can lead to the expression of outgroup bias, or a sense that the outgroup is better and therefore ought to be privileged. Thus system justification theory extends the social identity perspective to explain why inequality and discrimination amongst groups is perpetuated and tolerated.

While these theories underlying discrimination are by no means exhaustive of the social psychological literature, we believe that these approaches help explain why, how, and when discrimination occurs and is perpetuated over time. These theories thus offer a solid grounding from which to consider the studies of discrimination that follow.

Measuring Discrimination

The United States General Social Survey dropped its equal-employment-opportunity question because of near-unanimous support for the principle (Quillan, 2006). However, the evolution and predictive power of the theories just discussed speak to the fact that prejudice and discrimination, rather than evaporating in the heat of social change, remain strong and reliable features of intergroup life. There are overt and subtle ways to capture the impulses and evaluations that precede discrimination.

Explicit measures of prejudice are self-report measures in which the participants state their attitudes about, or action tendencies toward, a particular target. These measures presume that participants are conscious of their evaluations and behavioural tendencies, and are constructed in a way to reduce the amount of socially desirable responding. In meta-analyses of the relationship between explicit prejudice and discrimination, the authors found a modest correlation between the two ($r = .32$: Dovidio et al., 1996; $r=.36$: Greenwald et al., 2009). Despite the modest effect sizes, the fact that they are derived from studies conducted in a range of situations and intergroup contexts suggests the reliability of the relationships, and the value of explicit measures.

However, as our review of theories of discrimination suggests, biases do not necessarily have to be conscious or intentional to create unfair discrimination. Implicit measures of prejudice capture the evaluations and beliefs that are automatically, often unconsciously, activated by the presence or thought of the target group (Dovidio et al., 2001). These measures overcome the social desirability concerns that plague explicit measures because they allow us to capture prejudice that people may be unwilling and/or unable to express (Fazio and Olson, 2003). The Implicit Association Test (IAT) is an example of implicit measurement (Greenwald et al., 1998), that is based on the finding that people make connections more quickly between pairs of ideas that are already related in our minds. Thus, it should be more difficult, and hence take longer, to produce evaluatively incompatible than compatible responses. For example, in the case of ageism, people typically take longer to pair the words 'old' and 'good' than they do to pair the words 'old' and 'bad'. It is considered to be an instance of prejudice because it involves a bias in our minds such that there are stronger mental associations between stereotype-consistent features (typically negative) and particular groups than between stereotype-inconsistent features and group membership. The time taken to respond does not depend on any essential or accurate feature of the groups in question, but reflects well-learned cultural associations that automatically come to mind (Blair et al., 2004). In a meta-analysis of the relationship between implicit prejudice and discrimination, the authors found a weak-to-modest relationship ($r = .27$: Greenwald et al., 2009), though in the context of studies that dealt with Black-White relations in the US, the relationship between implicit measures and discrimination ($r = .24$) was stronger than that between explicit measures and discrimination ($r = .12$).

Experiments on unobtrusive forms of prejudice show that White bias against Blacks is more prevalent than indicated by surveys (Crosby et al., 1980). Despite people's best intentions, their ethnically biased cognitions and associations may persist. The result is a modern, subtle form of prejudice (that can be tapped by both implicit and explicit measures) that goes underground so as not to conflict with anti-racist norms while it continues to shape people's cognition, emotions and behaviours (Dovidio and Gaertner, 2004). Discrimination may take the form of blaming the outgroup for their disadvantage (Hewstone et al., 2002; Jost and Banaji, 1994; Pettigrew et al., 1998), not supporting policies that uplift outgroup members (Gilens, 1996), avoidance of interactions with outgroup members (Van Laar et al., 2005), automatically treating outgroup members as embodying stereotypical traits of their groups (Fiske, 1998), preference for the ingroup over outgroup leading to preferential reward allocation (Tajfel and Turner, 1986), and ambivalent responses to the outgroup, that is having mixed positive and negative views about outgroup members (Glick and Fiske, 1996) which can lead to avoidance and passive harm to the outgroup (Cuddy et al., 2007).

We now consider two empirical approaches – laboratory and field studies – to the study of discrimination and the processes that underlie it.

Laboratory Studies

In a laboratory study, the investigator manipulates a variable of interest, randomly assigns participants to different conditions of the variable or treatments, and measures their responses to the manipulation while attempting to control for other relevant conditions or attributes.

Laboratory studies can reveal both subtle and blatant discriminatory responses, and illuminate the processes that shape these responses. In a classic social psychological paper, Word et al. (1974) studied the presence and effects of subtle non-verbal discriminatory behaviours among university students in a series of two studies. In Study 1, they identified non-verbal discriminatory behaviours from White interviewers of Black versus White job applicants. In Study 2 they were able to demonstrate that such subtle discriminatory behaviours when directed against White applicants by White interviewers elicited behaviours stereotypically associated with Blacks, and led to poor performance in the interview, a demonstration of the self-fulfilling prophesy; i.e. treating others like they will fail causes them to fail. This study powerfully demonstrated that negative stereotypes about an outgroup can give rise to negative passive behaviour, which in turn can have performance-reducing consequences for the recipients of such non-verbal behaviours. In legal settings, negative verbal and non-verbal treatment may constitute unlawful discrimination when they result in the creation of a hostile work environment (Blank et al., 2004).

In an effort to examine the relationship between explicit and implicit measures of prejudice and verbal and non-verbal discriminatory behaviours, Dovidio et al. (2002) first asked White university student participants to complete a self-report measure of their attitudes towards Blacks. Some time later, during the experimental phase of the study, they subliminally primed participants with White and Black faces and positive and negative non-stereotypic characteristics which participants had to pair together. Subliminal priming refers to stimuli presented fleetingly, outside conscious awareness. Their response time to each category-word combination (e.g. black/ friendly) was measured as an indication of their implicit associations, with shorter response latencies reflecting higher implicit associations of particular ethnic groups with particular stereotypes. Then participants, who were told they were taking part in an unrelated study, engaged in an interaction task first with a White (Black) confederate and then with a Black (White) confederate; these interactions were videotaped. After each interaction, both the participant and the confederate completed rating scales of their own and the confederate's friendliness. In the next stage of the study, the videotaped interactions were played in silent mode to two judges who rated the friendliness of non-verbal behaviours of the participants. As the authors anticipated, the explicit prejudice measure significantly predicted bias in White participants' verbal behaviour to Black relative to White confederates. The implicit measure significantly predicted White participants' non-verbal friendliness and the extent to which the confederates and observers perceived bias in the participants' friendliness.

This study powerfully elucidates a point raised earlier in this chapter, that behaviours which some judge to be discriminatory will not be seen as such by others. Specifically, implicit negative attitudes towards the outgroup can lead majority/minority or advantaged/disadvantaged group members to form divergent impressions of their interaction partner. These implicit attitudes are associated in this study and in the one by Word et al. (1974) with non-verbal behaviours (what the BIAS map would term passive harm), which led to the development of self-fulfilling prophesies. The inconsistency of one's implicit and explicit attitudes explains why majority and minority group members experience interethnic interactions in such divergent ways; majority group members refer to their explicit attitudes when thinking about interactions with outgroup members, while minority group members seem to rely more on the majority group member's implicit attitude, as reflected in their non-verbal behaviours, to determine the friendliness of the interaction.

Consistent with the predictions of aversive racism, discrimination against Blacks in helping behaviours was more likely when participants could rationalise decisions not to help with reasons that had nothing to do with ethnicity. For example, using university students, Gaertner and Dovidio (1977) showed that in an emergency, Black victims were less likely to be helped when the participant had the opportunity to diffuse responsibility over several other people, who could potentially be called upon to help; however, Blacks and Whites were helped equally when the participant was the only bystander. In a meta-analysis on helping behaviours, Saucier et al. (2005) found that when helping was lengthier, riskier, more difficult, more effortful, and when potential helpers were further away from targets, Whites gave less help to Blacks than to fellow Whites.

Similar discrimination was evidenced when Dovidio and Gaertner (2000) studied how White university student participants made selection decisions in a hiring task. They found that White participants did not discriminate against White relative to Black candidates when the candidate's qualifications were either strong or weak, but did discriminate when the decision was more ambiguous (i.e. when qualifications were middling). Echoing findings from the helping studies, in the ambiguous condition, participants were able to find alternative explanations for their unwillingness to hire Black applicants, and thus could express their prejudice without having to be faced with it. This is a classic manifestation of modern or aversive racism (Dovidio and Gaertner, 2004; McConahay, 1986).

Another study with obvious real-world consequence is Blair et al.'s (2004) study on judge biases in criminal sentencing. The authors anticipated that moving beyond mere ethnic categorisation, further intra-category categorisation, specifically the possession of Afrocentric features, could predict behaviour towards members of subcategories. Afrocentric features refer to features deemed to be typical of African Americans: darker skin, fuller lips and broader noses (Pizzi et al., 2005). Afrocentric features vary between categories as well as within them, and it is well-documented that possession of Afrocentric features is likely to lead to greater categorisation as Black, which in turn is likely to lead to stereotypic inferences about that individual (Blair et al., 2002; Eberhardt et al., 2006).

Using data from the Department of Corrections in Florida, which has a webpage for every incarcerated inmate (including their criminal record, sentence and a court 'mug shot'), the authors conducted a study of the relationship between having Afrocentric features and sentence length. They used advanced law students to create an index of each felon's criminal history, which reflected aspects such as the seriousness of the current convicted offence and the number of prior offences. The Afrocentric features of each of the felons was rated by participants from earlier studies. There was evidence of longer sentences for those with the same criminal history if they were higher on Afrocentric features (within ethnic group). Particularly the authors found that controlling for criminal history and crime type, those with more Afrocentric features tended to have received a judicial sentence that was on average eight months longer than those with less Afrocentric features.

Related to the justice system, the final laboratory study that we will discuss is an important piece of research that involves split-second decisions with possibly fatal consequences. Correll et al. (2002) conducted several studies to understand whether implicit associations of ethnicity with certain group stereotypes might inform a police officer's decision to shoot a suspect. Using a simple videogame, Black or White targets holding guns or other non-threatening objects (such as mobile phones), appeared in real-world backgrounds. Participants (who included university students and adults from the wider population) were told to 'shoot' armed targets and to 'not shoot' unarmed targets. In line with their expectations, the authors found that White participants made the correct decision to shoot an armed target more quickly if the target was Black than if he was White. Conversely, they also found that White participants decided to 'not shoot' an unarmed target more quickly if he was White. What this study shows is that our implicit associations can have very grave consequences, and are particularly powerful predictors of behaviour in situations where we are required to react very quickly, and with little time for non-automatic processes to operate. This is once again a demonstration that 'best intentions', while very important in a range of domains, may sometimes be too difficult to access at times of emergency.

The authors also conducted a further study (Correll et al., 2007) in which they gave actual police officers the same response latency task. They found that police officers demonstrated bias in the latencies of their correct responses, in that the automatic associations come to mind for them as well. However, the police officers made many more correct decisions and their decisions were not influenced by the irrelevant cue of target ethnicity. This demonstrates the effect of training; the automatic associations were still there, but their impact on final performance could be controlled such that the officers did not act on this bias.

Field Studies

Laboratory experiments are well-suited to establishing cause-and-effect relationships (internal validity), but the often artificial nature of laboratory studies and their general reliance on college students as participants raise questions about the generalisability (external validity) of the findings. Field studies complement laboratory research because they observe people in their natural settings, or when they are in treatment and control conditions that are not created by the researcher. Field experiments measure the impact of differential treatments more cleanly than non-experimental approaches, yet they have the advantage of occurring in a realistic setting and hence are more directly generalisable than laboratory experiments. However they do often involve non-random allocation of participants to conditions, and do not give researchers the ability to control for possible confounding variables.

The role that prejudice plays in helping behaviours is illustrated by Bushman and Bonacci (2004) in their modern version of the lost-letter technique (Milgram et al., 1965). In this study, White student participants at an American university completed a self-report measure of prejudice towards Arabs. Then two weeks later, they 'mistakenly' received an email intended for another student (who was of Arab or European descent) containing information that the intended recipient either won a prestigious scholarship or was not awarded it. The winner of the scholarship needed to respond to the email within 48 hours in order to receive the scholarship. Of interest was whether the student alerted the sender to the mistake. The authors found that when the recipient won the scholarship worth thousands of dollars, more prejudiced participants were less likely to alert the sender if the recipient was of Arab rather than European descent. If, however, the intended recipient did not win the scholarship, then more prejudiced participants were more likely to alert the sender if the non-winning recipient was of Arab rather than European descent. Thus the prejudiced participants were less likely to pass on time-sensitive and highly important good news, but more likely to pass on bad news that was not time-sensitive. Other paradigms studying the effects of prejudice on behaviour gauge willingness to help a caller who has just spent his/her last dime mistakenly calling the recipient of the call (though in the age of cell phones, the utility of this paradigm is quite limited!), someone who drops papers or books, or knocks over a cup of pencils (see Crosby et al., 1980).

Hiring decisions also have their counterpart in field studies. Glick et al. (1988) examined gender discrimination in hiring by asking professionals to evaluate bogus résumés of men and women for jobs that were either masculine or feminine in nature. The individuating information provided about male and female job applicants led participants to make virtually identical inferences about the personality traits of male and female applicants who had the same information in their résumés. However, even though a 'masculine' female applicant was perceived to be just as aggressive, independent, strong, and decisive as a 'masculine' male applicant, the female applicant was less likely to be interviewed or hired for the male-dominated job of sales manager. Similarly, female applicants were consistently preferred over male applicants for the job of receptionist or secretary, even when the applicants were thought not to differ in the degree to which they possessed masculine or feminine personality traits. The authors argue that one possibility is that employers consider certain occupations to be gendered and thus hire on the basis of that stereotype rather than on the basis of individuating non-gendered information about the applicant. Thus gender plays a disproportionate role in explaining hiring preferences for gendered occupations.

Prejudice and discrimination do not always manifest in more/less likelihood of being hired, but they do have other more subtle manifestations, consistent with findings from Word et al. (1974). Hebl et al. (2002) had confederate 'applicants' (blind to their condition) wear hats labelled with either 'gay and proud' (stigmatising condition) or 'Texan and proud' (neutral condition) and apply for retail jobs. The results revealed that gay and lesbian applicants did *not* experience formal discrimination (i.e. no differences in being told there were jobs available, being able to fill out applications, or in receiving job callbacks) relative to assumed heterosexual applicants, but they did experience more subtle and informal discrimination (the average interaction length was 6 1/2 minutes with non-stigmatised applicants, compared to about 4 minutes for the gay and lesbian applicants, and the interactions were also rated by observers as having less warmth, increased interaction distance and more rudeness) than did assumed heterosexual applicants.

Doctor–patient interactions are a realm in which we do not expect to see high levels of ethnic prejudice or discrimination, as the disease is expected to serve as a common and uniting enemy. Penner et al. (2010b) studied the effects of physician bias in interactions between Black patients and non-Black physicians in a primary care facility in the US. The patient participants completed a questionnaire on their health, perceived discrimination, and compliance with medical regimens, while the physician participants completed measures of their explicit and implicit bias. The interactions between physician and patient were recorded, and then after the interaction, the patients' and physicians' immediate and longer-term reactions to the interactions were recorded. The patients had a less positive view of interactions and talked less (see also Penner et al., 2010a) with physicians who were low in explicit prejudice and high in implicit prejudice than they did with physicians who had any other combination of implicit and explicit prejudice. Low explicit-high implicit prejudice physicians represent the classic aversive racist, and Black patients may have responded to these types of physicians most negatively because of the dissonance between the physician's view of themselves (possibly in terms of verbal behaviour) and their actual (likely non-verbal) behaviours which betrayed their implicit prejudice.

Other studies suggest that discrimination may also be responsible for disparities in cancer treatments (Penner et al., in press). For example, Black women are more likely than White women to receive inappropriately low doses of chemotherapy for breast cancer; and Black men are less likely than White men to receive aggressive or definitive treatment for moderate and advanced grades of prostate cancer. Neither of these kinds of difference were explained by medical reasons or factors such as the availability of medical insurance. These and other studies of Black–White health disparities in the US demonstrate the potentially serious consequences of expressing prejudice and experiencing discrimination, even in what is commonly regarded as a prejudice-transcending domain such as healthcare.

Consequences of Discrimination

The consequences of discrimination are pervasive, cumulative and long-lasting, and in this section we will consider some of these.

In terms of the effects of discrimination on neighbourhood choice, it has been argued that many people occupy segregated areas because of discrimination by members of the majority group, who prefer not to share neighbourhoods with minority members and newcomers (Cater and Hones, 1978). Thus particular groups often live encapsulated in enclaves (Peach, 1996), attached to the economy, but separate from the broader society (Modood et al., 1997). This segregated living has clear consequences for integration, and the absence of positive intergroup contact is associated with greater prejudice (Hewstone and Brown, 1986).

Discrimination across situations and time can give rise to cumulative disadvantage. Avoidance may appear harmless in any given situation but, when aggregated across situations, such rejection can lead to long-term exclusion. This is particularly problematic in situations where social networking matters (Heath and McMahon, 1997), such as employment, education, and health care. Such exclusionary practices can be just as damaging as more active and direct discrimination. In addition to discrimination across situations, cumulative disadvantage can also arise from exclusion across group memberships. Situations of 'multiple jeopardy' arise when people are denied access on the basis of more than one of their memberships (e.g. a homosexual black woman in a wheelchair). Individuals who are in double or triple minority or stigmatised groups experience considerable difficulty in being accepted as equal members of society (Crisp and Hewstone, 1999), and in succeeding. Cumulative disadvantage also arises from persistent disadvantage. For minority group members, today's outcomes may affect the incentives for tomorrow's behaviour at every stage of the life cycle and in different social domains (Loury, 2000; Lundberg and Startz, 1998). This leads to entrenched social hierarchies and reduced social mobility.

Another consequence of discrimination, either verbal or nonverbal (and demonstrated by several of the studies discussed), is that it can result in under-performance and stress. Others' negative stereotypes and expectations of the discriminated-against group can lead one to experience stereotype threat, which is a debilitating concern that one will be evaluated on the basis of the negative stereotype (Steele and Aronson, 1995). This has been shown to be related to under-performance in educational settings (Steele and Aronson, 1995) and also employment settings (Darley and Gross, 1983; Word, et al., 1974), in the form of lower organisational commitment, career commitment, organisational self-esteem and job satisfaction (Ragins and Cornwell, 2002). It is also associated with increased anxiety, stress and poor physical health for targets (Waldo, 1999).

In addition to increases in anxiety, being discriminated against can have implications for other aspects of mental wellbeing (Pascoe and Richman, 2009). In a multilevel study using a Black sample of 10-12 year old children in the US, Simons et al. (2002) found that a history of discrimination had an impact on depressive symptoms at both the individual and community level. At the individual-level, in addition to uninvolved parenting and criminal victimisation, having a history of being personally racially discriminated against explained childhood depressive symptoms. At the community-level, a history of discrimination was associated with depressive symptoms over and above criminal victimisation and ethnic identification. One way in which the stigmatised regulate emotion and protect self-esteem in the face of threats to their identity is by withdrawing their efforts from and/or disengaging their self-esteem from domains in which they are negatively stereotyped or fear being a target of discrimination (Major et al., 1998; Steele, 1997). For example, women who were primed with negative gender stereotypes chose to answer fewer math questions and focused instead on verbal questions in a challenging test (Davies et al., 2002).

While discrimination and stereotype threat can lead stigmatised group members to underperform, an additional implication is that members of a disadvantaged group may need to become better qualified than majority group members in order to succeed (Biernat and Kobrynowicz, 1997). This is due to a perception that on average, members of stigmatised groups are poorly qualified and incompetent. Thus members of the lower-status groups are taxed for their group membership, by perceiving that they need to work harder than advantaged group members in order to succeed. This is sometimes referred to in American common parlance as the 'Black tax'.

Perceived discrimination is also closely connected with 'race-based rejection sensititivity' (Mendoza-Denton et al., 2002). This refers to the anxiety that minority/stigmatised group members experience of being rejected purely on account of their ethnicity/group membership. Mendoza-Denton et al. (2002) found that Black students high in race-based rejection sensitivity had fewer White friends and interacted with professors and teaching assistants less compared to students low in race-based rejection sensitivity.

Finally, with regard to health outcomes, the racially discordant nature of most medical interactions (about 75 per cent of all US medical interactions with Black patients involve non-Black physicians) appears to have deleterious consequences. Specifically, they result in interactions that are, relative to racially concordant interactions, less patient-centred, characterised by less positive affect, involve less patient participation in decision making, more likely to be dominated by the physician and involve poorer information exchange between physician and patient (Penner, et al., in press). This, combined with a history of discrimination, can lead to very negative health outcomes for minority group patients. In a longitudinal study Penner and his colleagues (Penner et al., 2009) showed that Black patients who reported experiencing high levels of discrimination were less likely to adhere to the treatment prescribed to them by non-Black physicians, and to have more negative reactions to these physicians. They also reported poorer health and, in fact, their medical records showed that they had more chronic diseases.

Conclusion

The foregoing offers an insight into the social psychological theories, measurement and consequences of discrimination. Implicit and explicit measurement of prejudice and discrimination illustrate that they abound, and are of great consequence.

However, having prejudice does not mean that individuals will necessarily engage in discriminatory behaviours. As discussed, the meta-analyses reported (Dovidio et al., 1996; Greenwald et al., 2009) found a modest relationship between implicit and explicit measures and discrimination-related tendencies. This suggests that while prejudice is one of the roots of discrimination, not all individuals who hold negative attitudes go on to discriminate, and that other variables have significant explanatory power. Furthermore, particularly with regard to predictions based on implicit measures, they do not take into account the other forces that operate upon an individual in a social setting. The strong norms of equal opportunity, profit motivation and job and diversity training might motivate an individual or an organisation to behave in non-discriminatory ways (Correll, et al., 2007), and not merely to be negatively influenced by their implicit associations (Mitchell and Tetlock, 2008), and even explicit evaluations.

What is clear beyond the shadow of a doubt is that discrimination has very grave consequences for minority group and stigmatised individuals and that the disadvantage experienced by any one group in any one generation can have a multiplier effect on intergenerational disadvantage across domains, situations and group memberships. Thus more research is needed to uncover the many manifestations of discrimination and its processes, and to understand the ways in which it might effectively be reduced or prevented. We hope to have demonstrated that social psychologists have made some important inroads in this effort, and the other chapters in the volume have provided excellent insights from other disciplines. Greater clarity and faster advancement will be achieved through cross-disciplinary collaboration.

References

Al Ramiah, A., Hewstone, M. and Schmid, K. (in press). 'Self, identity and society'. *Psychological Studies*.

Barnett, E. and Halverson, J. (2001). 'Local increases in coronary heart disease mortality among Blacks and Whites in the United States, 1985-1995'. *American Journal of Public Health, 91*, 1499-1506.

Biernat, M. and Kobrynowicz, D. (1997). 'Gender- and race-based standards of competence: Lower minimum standards but higher ability standards for devalued groups'. *Journal of Personality and Social Psychology, 72*, 544-557.

Blair, I.V., Judd, C. M. and Chapleau, K.M. (2004). 'The influence of afrocentric facial features in criminal sentencing'. *Psychological Science, 15*, 674-679.

Blair, I.V., Judd, C.M., Sadler, M.S. and Jenkins, C. (2002). 'The role of Afrocentric features in person perception: Judging by features and categories'. *Journal of Personality and Social Psychology, 83*, 5-25.

Blank, R.M., Dabady, M. and Citro, C.F. (eds.) (2004). *Measuring Racial Discrimination* Washington, DC: The National Academies Press.

Bobo, L. (2001). 'Racial attitudes and relations at the close of the twentieth century'. In N. Smelser, W.J. Wilson and F. Mitchell (eds.), *America Becoming: Racial Trends and Their Consequences* (pp. 262-299). Washington, DC: National Academy Press.

Bushman, B.J. and Bonacci, A.M. (2004). 'You've got mail: Using e-mail to examine the effect of prejudiced attitudes on discrimination against Arabs'. *Journal of Experimental Social Psychology, 40*, 753-759.

Cater, J. and Hones, T. (1978). 'Ethnic and residential space: The case of Asians in Bradford'. *Tijdscrift voor Economische en Sociale Geografie, 70*, 86-97.

Cohen, G.L., Garcia, J., Apfel, N. and Master, A. (2006). 'Reducing the racial achievement gap: A social-psychological intervention'. *Science, 313*, 1307-1310.

Correll, J., Judd, C.M., Park, B. and Wittenbrink, B. (2010). 'Measuring prejudice, stereotypes and discrimination'. In J.F. Dovidio, M. Hewstone, P. Glick and V.M. Esses (eds.), *The Sage Handbook of Prejudice, Stereotyping, and Discrimination*. Thousand Oaks, CA: Sage.

Correll, J., Park, B., Judd, C.M. and Wittenbrink, B. (2002). 'The police officer's dilemma: Using ethnicity to disambiguate potentially threatening individuals'. *Journal of Personality and Social Psychology, 83*, 1314-1329.

Correll, J., Park, B., Judd, C.M., Wittenbrink, B., Sadler, M.S. and Keesee, T. (2007). 'Across the thin blue line: Police officers and racial bias in the decision to shoot'. *Journal of Personality and Social Psychology, 92*, 1006-1023.

Crandall, C.S., Eshleman, A. and O'Brien, L.T. (2002). 'Social norms and the expression and suppression of prejudice: The struggle for internalization'. *Journal of Personality and Social Psychology, 82*, 359-378.

Crisp, R.J. and Hewstone, M. (1999). 'Differential evaluation of crossed category groups: Patterns, processes, and reducing intergroup bias'. *Group Processes and Intergroup Relations, 2*, 303-333.

Crosby, F., Bromley, S. and Saxe, L. (1980). Recent unobtrusive studies of Black and White discrimination and prejudice: A literature review. *Psychological Bulletin, 87*, 546-563.

Cuddy, A.J.C., Fiske, S.T, and Glick, P. (2007). 'The BIAS map: Behaviors from intergroup affect and stereotypes'. *Journal of Personality and Social Psychology, 92*, 631-648.

Darley, J.M., and Fazio, R.H. (1980). 'Expectancy confirmation processes arising in the social interaction sequence'. *American Psychologist, 35*, 867-881.

Darley, J.M. and Gross, P.H. (1983). 'A hypothesis-confirming bias in labeling effects'. *Journal of Personality and Social Psychology, 44*, 20-33.

Davies, P.G., Spencer, S.J., Quinn, D.M. and Gerhardstein, R. (2002). 'Consuming images: How television commercials that elicit stereotype threat can restrain women academically and professionally'. *Personality and Social Psychology Bulletin, 28*, 1615-1628.

Dovidio, J.F., Brigham, J.C., Johnson, B.T. and Gaertner, S.L. (1996). 'Stereotyping, prejudice, and discrimination: Another look'. In N. Macrae, C. Stangor and M. Hewstone (eds.), *Stereotypes and Stereotyping* (pp. 276-319). New York: Guilford.

Dovidio, J.F. and Gaertner, S.L. (2000). 'Aversive racism in selection decisions: 1989 and 1999'. *Psychological Science, 11*, 315-319.

Dovidio, J.F. and Gaertner, S.L. (2004). 'Aversive racism'. In M. Zanna (ed.), *Advances in experimental social psychology* (pp. 1-52). San Diego, CA: Academic Press.

Dovidio, J.F., Kawakami, K. and Beach, K. (2001). 'Examination of the relationship between implicit and explicit measures of intergroup attitudes'. In R. Brown and S. Gaertner (eds.), *Intergroup relations: Blackwell handbook in social psychology* (Vol. Intergroup relations (pp. 175-197). Oxford: Blackwell. , pp. 175-197). Oxford Blackwell.

Dovidio, J.F., Kawakami, K. and Gaertner, S.L. (2002). 'Implicit and explicit prejudice and interracial interaction'. *Journal of Personality and Social Psychology, 82*, 62-28.

Eberhardt, J.L., Davies, P.G., Purdie-Vaughns, V.J. and Johnson, S.L. (2006). 'Looking deathworthy: Perceived stereotypicality of Black defendants predicts capital-sentencing outcomes'. *Psychological Science, 17*, 383-386.

Fazio, R.H. and Olson, M.A. (2003). 'Implicit measures in social cognition research: Their meaning and use'. *Annual Review of Psychology, 54*.

Fiske, S.T. (1998). 'Stereotyping, prejudice, and discrimination'. In D. Gilbert, S.T. Fiske and G. Lindzey (eds.), *Handbook of Social Psychology* (4 ed., Vol. 2, pp. 357-411). Boston, MA: McGraw-Hill.

Fiske, S.T., Cuddy, A.J.C., Glick, P. and Xu, J. (2002). 'A model of (often mixed) stereotype content: Competence and warmth respectively follow from status and competition'. *Journal of Personality and Social Psychology*, 878-902.

Gaertner, S.L. and Dovidio, J.F. (1977). 'The subtlety of white racism, arousal and helping behavior'. *Journal of Personality and Social Psychology, 35*, 691-707.

Gaertner, S.L. and Dovidio, J.F. (1986) 'The aversive form of racism' in J.F. Dovidio and S.L. Gaertner (eds.) *Prejudice, Discrimination and Racism*. Orlando, FL: Academic Press.

Gilens, M. (1996). 'Race coding and white opposition to welfare'. *American Political Science Review, 90*, 593-604.

Glick, P. and Fiske, S.T. (1996). The Ambivalent Sexism Inventory: Differentiating hostile and benevolent sexism. *Journal of Personality and Social Psychology, 70*, 491-512.

Glick, P., Zion, C. and Nelson, C. (1988). 'What mediates sex discrimination in hiring decisions?' *Journal of Personality and Social Psychology*, 55, 178-186.

Goldman, B., Gutek, B., Stein, J. and Lewis, K. (2006). 'Antecedents and consequences of employment discrimination in organizations'. *Journal of Management*, 32, 786-830.

Greenwald, A.G., McGhee, D.E. and Schwartz, J.K.L. (1998). 'Measuring individual differences in implicit cognition: The Implicit Association Test'. *Journal of Personality and Social Psychology*, 74, 1464-1480.

Greenwald, A.G., Poehlman, T.A., Uhlmann, E.L. and Banaji, M.R. (2009). 'Understanding and using the Implicit Association Test: III. Meta-analysis of predictive validity'. *Journal of Persoanlity and Social Psychology*, 97, 17-41.

Heath, A.F. and McMahon, D. (1997). *Education and occupational attainment: the impact of ethnic origins*. London: HMSO.

Hebl, M., Foster, J.M., Mannix, L.M. and Dovidio, J.F. (2002). 'Formal and interpersonal discrimination: A field study examination of applicant bias'. *Personality and Social Psychological Bulletin*, 28, 815-825.

Hewstone, M., and Brown, R. (1986). 'Contact is not enough: An intergroup perspective on the "contact hypothesis"'. In M. Hewstone and R. Brown (eds.), *Contact and conflict in intergroup encounters* (pp. 1-44). Oxford, UK: Blackwell.

Hewstone, M., Rubin, M. and Willis, H. (2002). 'Intergroup bias'. *Annual Review of Psychology*, 53, 575-604.

Hume, D. (1939). *A Treatise of Human Nature*. Oxford: Oxford University Press.

Jost, J.T. and Banaji, M.R. (1994). 'The role of stereotyping in system-justification and the production of false consciousness'. *British Journal of Social Psychology* 33, 1-27.

Jost, J.T. and Burgess, D. (2000). 'Attitudinal ambivalence and the conflict between group and system justification motives in low status groups'. *Personality and Social Psychology Bulletin* 26, 293-305.

Jost, J.T., Burgess, D. and Mosso, C. (2001). 'Conflicts of legitimation among self, group, and system: The integrative potential of system justification theory'. In J.T. Jost and B. Major (eds.), *The psychology of legitimacy: Emerging perspectives on ideology, justice, and intergroup relations* (pp. 363-388). New York: Cambridge University Press.

Katz, I. and Hass, R.G. (1988). 'Racial ambivalence and American value conflict: Correlational and priming studies of dual cognitive structures'. *Journal of Personality and Social Psychology, 55*, 893-905.

Loury, G.C. (2000). 'Social exclusion and ethnic groups: The challenge to economics'. *Boston University – Institute for Economic Development, 106.*

Lundberg, S. and Startz, R. (1998). 'Inequality and race: Models and policy'. *Working Papers 0067.*

Major, B., Spencer, S., Schmader, T., Wolfe, C. and Crocker, J. (1998). 'Coping with negative stereotypes about intellectual performance: The role of psychological disengagement'. *Personality and Social Psychology Bulletin, 24,* 34-50.

McConahay, J.B. (1986). Modern racism, ambivalence, and the modern racism scale. In S.L. Gaertner and J.F. Dovidio (eds.), *Prejudice, discrimination and racism* (pp. 91-125). London: Academic Press.

Mendoza-Denton, R., Downey, G., Purdie, V.J., Davis, A. and Pietrzak, J. (2002). 'Sensitivity to status-based rejection: Implications for African American students' college experience'. *Journal of Personality and Social Psychology, 83,* 896-918.

Milgram, S., Mann, L. and Harter, S. (1965). 'The lost letter technique: A tool of social research'. *Public Opinion Quarterly, 29,* 437–438.

Mitchell, G. and Tetlock, P.E. (2008). 'Calibrating Prejudice in Milliseconds'. *Social Psychology Quarterly, 71,* 12-16.

Modood, T., Berthoud, R., Lakey, J., Nazroo, J., Smith, P., Virdee, S., et al. (1997). 'Ethnic Minorities in Britain: Diversity and Disadvantage' *Fourth National Survey of Ethnic Minorities.*

Pascoe, E.A. and Richman, L.S. (2009) 'Perceived discrimination and health: A meta-analytic review'. *Psychological Bulletin,* 135, 531-554.

Peach, C. (1996). 'The meaning of segregation'. *Planning Practice and Research, 11,* 137-150.

Penner, L.A., Dovidio, J.F., Edmondson, D., Dailey, R., Markova, T., Albrecht, T. L., et al. (2009). 'The experience of discrimination, and black-white health disparities in medical care'. *Journal of Black Psychology, 35,* 180-203.

Penner, L.A., Dovidio, J.F., West, T.V., Gaertner, S.L., Albrecht, T.L., Daily, R. K. et al. (2010a). 'Aversive racism and medical interactions with Black patients: A field study'. Paper presented at the Annual Meeting of Society of Behavioral Medicine, Seattle, Washington,

Penner, L.A., Dovidio, J.F., West, T.V., Gaertner, S.L., Albrecht, T.L., Daily, R.K. et al. (2010b). 'Aversive racism and medical interactions with Black patients: A field study'. *Journal of Experimental Social Psychology, 46*, 436-440.

Penner, L.A., Eggly, S., Griggs, J., Orom, H. and Underwood, W. I. (in press). Life-threatening disparities: The roles of ethnicity and social class in the treatment of cancer. *Journal of Social Issues*

Pettigrew, T.F., Jackson, J.S., Ben Brika, J., Lemaine, G., Meertens, R.W., Wagner, U. et al. (1998). 'Outgroup prejudice in Western Europe'. *European Review of Social Psychology, 8*, 241-273.

Pettigrew, T.F. and Tropp, L.R. (2006). 'A meta-analytic test of intergroup contact theory'. *Journal of Personality and Social Psychology, 90*, 751-783

Pizzi, W., Blair, I. and Judd, C. (2005). 'Discrimination in sentencing based on Afro-centric features'. *Michigan Journal of Race and Law, 10*, 1-27.

Quillan, L. (2006). 'New approaches to understanding racial prejudice and discrimination'. *Annual Review of Sociology, 32*, 299-328.

Ragins, B.R., and Cornwell, J.M. (2002). 'Pink triangles: Antecedents and consequences of perceived workplace discrimination against gay and lesbian employees'. *Journal of Applied Psychology, 86*, 1244-1261.

Saucier, D.A., Miller, C.T. and Doucet, N. (2005). 'Differences in helping whites and blacks: A meta-analysis'. *Personality and Social Psychology Review, 9*, 2-16.

Sidanius, J. and Pratto, F. (1999). *Social dominance: An intergroup theory of social hierarchy and oppression*. NY: Cambridge University Press.

Simons, R.L., Murry, V., McLoyd, V., Lin, K.-H., Cutrona, C. and Conger, R.D. (2002). 'Discrimination, crime, ethnic identity, and parenting as correlates of depressive symptoms among African American children: A multilevel analysis'. *Development and Psychopathology, 14*, 371-393.

Steele, C.M. (1997). 'A threat in the air: How stereotypes shape intellectual identity and performance'. *American Psychologist, 52*, 613-629.

Steele, C.M., and Aronson, J. (1995). 'Stereotype threat and the intellectual test performance of African Americans'. *Journal of Personality and Social Psychology, 69*, 797-811.

Steffensmeier, D. and Demuth, S. (2000). 'Ethnicity and Sentencing Outcomes in U.S. Federal Courts: Who is Punished More Harshly?' *American Sociological Review, 65*, 705-729.

Tajfel, H. and Turner, J.C. (1979). 'An integrative theory of intergroup conflict'. In S. Worchel and W.G. Austin (eds.), *The social psychology of intergroup relations* (pp. 33-47). Monterey, CA: Brooks Cole.

Tajfel, H., and Turner, J. C. (1986). 'The social identity theory of intergroup behavior'. In S. Worchel and W.G. Austin (eds.), *Psychology of intergroup relations* (pp. 7-24). Chicago: Nelson-Hall.

Turner, J.C. (1978). 'Social comparison, similarity and ingroup favouritism'. In T.H (ed.), *Differentiation between Social Groups: Studies in the Social Psychology of Intergroup Relations* (pp. 235-250). London: Academic Press.

Turner, J.C., Hogg, M.A., Oakes, P.J., Reicher, S.D. and Wetherell, M.S. (1987). *Rediscovering the social group*. Oxford, England: Basil Blackwell.

Underwood, W., De Monner, S., Ubel, P., Fagerlin, A., Sanda, M.G., and Wei, J.T. (2004). 'Racial/ethnic disparities in the treatment of localized/regional prostate cancer'. *The Journal of Urology, 171*, 1504-1507.

Van Laar, C., Levin, S., Sinclair, S. and Sidanius, J. (2005). 'The effect of college roommate contact on ethnic attitudes and behaviors'. *Journal of Experimental Social Psychology, 41*, 329-345.

Waldo, C.R. (1999). 'Working in a majority context: A structural model of heterosexism as minority stress in the workplace'. *Journal of Counseling Psychology, 46*, 218–232.

Word, C.O., Zanna, M.P. and Cooper, J. (1974). 'The nonverbal mediation of self-fulfilling prophecies in interracial interaction'. *Journal of Experimental Social Psychology, 10*, 109-120.

Chapter 6

Racism and Colorism in Post-Racial Societies

William Darity Jr

In 1995 a study was reported in the *Washington Post* newspaper, based upon a national survey jointly conducted by the *Post*, the Henry J. Kaiser Foundation and Harvard University (Morin, 1995). This study was conducted during the heart of the years of the Clinton Presidency, and it indicated that most of those individuals surveyed, regardless of race, greatly overestimated the number of minority Americans in the United States. Most whites, blacks, Hispanics and Asian Americans said that the black population, which constituted about 12 per cent share of the US population based on US census figures, had twice that share. On average, respondents said that the US black population was about one-quarter of the entire US population. Moreover, whites, blacks and Hispanics typically said that whites were less than half of the United States population, making them a numerical minority group as well. Of course the census data for 1995 indicated that whites were 73 per cent of the US population.

One woman, who had asserted that whites were a minority in the United States, when told that the census estimates indicated otherwise, responded that the census had to be wrong. Interviewees also were asked whether the average black was faring

better, worse or much the same as the average white with respect to income, jobs, housing, education, job security and access to health care. Government statistics at the time indicated
that blacks significantly lagged behind whites in all five of these
areas.

In the study, the researchers established criteria for distin-
guishing between who their most informed respondents were
and their least informed respondents. The most informed respondents were those who got five or more responses correct
that were related to these comparisons in the relative status of
blacks and whites. And the least informed were those who got
five or more incorrect. Among white respondents, only 22 per
cent of whites fell into the most informed category, 38 per cent
in the least informed category, with 40 per cent lying in between.

The issue that emerged in this study was one of gross and
widespread misperception of the demographic realities and the
relative conditions of groups that live in the United States. Also
interesting and disturbing was the connection to a set of political positions associated with these misperceptions. For example,
among whites who favoured cuts in the US food stamp programme, 34 per cent were in the most informed category. But
among the least informed, 62 per cent wanted cuts in food
stamps. And with respect to reducing aid to urban areas of the
United States, 48 per cent of the most informed wanted aid to
be reduced to urban areas in the United States, while 58 per cent
of the least informed wanted aid to be reduced.

This type of study was repeated in 2001, with very similar results. Half of all whites believed that blacks and whites had similar levels of education, although government statistics indicated
that 88 per cent of whites actually had completed high school in
the United States, versus 79 per cent of blacks among persons 25
years of age or older. Furthermore, 28 per cent of whites had actually completed university against 17 per cent of blacks. Never-

theless, half of all white respondents believed that there were no educational differences between blacks and whites.

Richard Morin, the *Washington Post* reporter who had written the original story about the 1995 study, made the following observation:

> The result suggests that there is an overwhelming sense among whites, that in 2001, we could not possibly be saddled with segregation and discrimination. And therefore things can't possibly be as bad as black Americans say they are.

Indeed, half of the white respondents believed that the average black was as well off as the average white in terms of the types of jobs they had and also in terms of job access. Again, based on government statistics, one-third of whites, in fact, held professional or managerial jobs versus slightly more than one-fifth of black Americans. Moreover, the jobless rate in the United States is generally twice as high for blacks as whites. In 2001, when the survey was conducted, the white unemployment rate was under 4 per cent in the United States while the black unemployment rate was above 8 per cent. And today in the midst of the Great Recession, the white unemployment rate approaches 9 per cent while the black unemployment rate is in excess of 15 per cent. This gap is what I view as one of the most acute indices of the persistence of discrimination in US labour markets.

It strikes me that the type of data that can be extracted from the US Census reinforces the vital role of public sector statistics. They must be unimpeachable in quality because they provide a register of accuracy not present in public opinion and public beliefs. But, clearly, developing good statistics is not enough. Creating wider awareness and conversation about their implications also is essential. Important data exists in the US that is inconsistent with widely held beliefs, but that data does not come before the public eye. Unfortunately, it is also often the case that misperception is heavily freighted by ideology, including pre-conceived beliefs – sometimes held by researchers themselves – that might inhibit their willingness to do the work needed to paint a more accurate picture. Indeed, my own discipline, economics, bears a special guilt in this regard.

The Doctrine of Post-Raciality

Economists en masse have long explicitly or implicitly embraced the trope of what I refer to as the doctrine of post-raciality. Post-raciality depicts a society that is devoid of discrimination and racism, one where the only remaining racists are folks who deign to even talk about race, where ethnic identities and so-called identity politics are wicked nationalisms that are anachronistic at best, and where all positions in society are obtained purely on the basis of merit.

I contend that conventional economics supports this trope of post-raciality in two major ways. First, more than virtually all other disciplines in the social sciences, economics embraces methodological individualism. Economists anchor their analysis on the individual as the decision maker, as the primary unit of human agency, not a racial or ethnic group, not social class, not nationality, but the individual as an autonomous decision making unit. When economists study groups at all, most still are inclined to start with individual motivation and behaviour. The second reason why economists tend to gravitate towards the doctrine of post-raciality is because economists widely believe – incorrectly – that market competition drives out discriminatory practices.

After all, discriminatory practices are characterised as being unprofitable; therefore, discriminatory wage differentials, should not be able to persist over time because, ostensibly, they do not make money for their practitioners. Profits and prejudice are treated as mutually exclusive and in that dichotomy profits win.

So, from that perspective, if we observe gaps in wages between descriptively marked groups, it must be because there are palpable differences in capacity to perform. There must be differences in individual productivity or differences in merit on average across the two groups.

So, why might members of two groups have different average levels of capacity to perform based upon these differentials in human capital? One could invoke either comparatively malign or comparatively benign explanations. First, let me mention two of the more malign explanations, then I will come to a more benign explanation – and then we will really get down to business. The first of the two more malign explanations is that these two groups might have differences on average in ability based upon differences in their respective genetic inheritances. This is precisely the kind of argument that Herrnstein and Murray made in their book *The Bell Curve* in the mid-1990s, and it seems to be exactly the type of argument the excessively ubiquitous John Derbyshire (2009) runs around making today. The second type of malign argument is that the kinds of group differences that result in wage gaps are attributable to cultural dysfunction on the part of one group or the other. This is the type of argument that is made by the University of Pennsylvania law professor Amy Wax (2009).

A third perspective – which I would suggest is more benign than the first two I have mentioned – is to argue that there is a pattern of historical deprivation that lies at the heart of average productivity differences across the groups. In a sense, one of the groups is comparatively undeveloped. I attribute this type of argument to Glenn Loury (2002).

These are the core arguments under post-racial doctrine: to the extent that we observe any ongoing differences in groups, it is not because of structural practices and processes that occur on a societal level – it is because of some sort of deficiency internal to the group that has less. So, under this type of post-racial imaging, current or ongoing racism or current ethnic chauvinism is not of significance in explaining persistent gaps.

My personal project is – and has been for many years – to try to re-establish what I think is in the data, in the evidence, that current racism and ethnic chauvinism play a very, very significant role in explaining the group-linked disparities that we continue observe in societies throughout the world.

My objective has been to break economics out of what I perceive as a narrow lane of thinking, since the evidence does not support that narrow lane of thinking. About five years ago, I began to grasp with several colleagues that our research programme had developed a certain coherence. At that time, I named what we were doing stratification economics (Darity 2005).

The Stratification Economics Research Programme

Stratification economics takes from sociology and social psychology the notion of the centrality of the group in human communities. The group becomes the primary unit of analysis; it is the source of identity, belonging, resources, norms and customs that might be embraced or rebelled against. Group identification can be assessed in at least two ways: it can be predicated on self-classification or social classification. Consequently, for a stratification economist, it is important to pay close attention in whichever data set we are using to whether respondents were given open-ended questions to answer about their racial or ethnic identity or whether they are given a pre-determined list from which they are asked to tick off a box to indicate their race or ethnicity.

It is also critical whether it is the respondent who is providing the answer to the identity question or whether the interviewer is providing the answer. If the respondent is providing it, then we can describe that as some sort of process of self-identification or self-classification. On the other hand, if the interviewer is providing it, this comes closer to capturing a process of social identification or social classification. Thus, what stratification economics has taken from sociology and social psychology is the critical role of the group and identity formation.

Stratification economics takes from economics what Herbert Simon (1976) once called 'substantive rationality'. Rational self-interest is the factor that animates the action of the group as a collectivity. Hence, stratification economists view the world as a place in which there are multiple self-interested groups as sites of identity that act with and against one another. That leads, in turn, to a body of projects or individual research activities that I find somewhat inspirational and vital to ongoing developments in the arena of the study of inter-group inequality.

The first is research that demonstrates that there are material benefits of racism to some groups. Instead of treating prejudice and profits as being antithetical, this body of work focuses on trying to establish that there actually could be sympathy for the devil. A second body of research focuses more heavily on wealth inequality than income or employment based inequality. Much of the work that has been done in economics and sociology for many years has focused on labour markets as sources of income through earnings, and has looked at those types of disparities as being central to understanding pecuniary inequalities. Only recently, perhaps in the last 10 to 15 years, prompted in part by the contributions of sociologists Oliver and Shapiro (1995), has much more attention been drawn to the question of intergroup wealth inequality.

Generally, wealth inequality is far wider and more disparate than income inequality. And group-linked differences in wealth are perhaps far more important in many societies, including the United States, than group-linked differences in income. In fact, I would argue that you cannot understand the overall distribution of wealth in most countries without paying close attention to the racial or ethnic distribution of wealth. Thus, another facet of the research agenda in stratification economics is to pay much closer attention to wealth disparities and how they connect with various groups.

A third facet of the research program in stratification economics is to look at differential group-linked outcomes in achievement and attainment in schooling. It is of particular importance to address the phenomenon of differential patterns of assignment of children to slow learner classes, depending upon the ethnic or racial group to which they belong. Also, in the US context, we have a body of instruction that is referred to as a gifted and talented curriculum. This is an accelerated learning curriculum and it is noteworthy how the racial and ethnic composition of participation in those types of curricula plays out *within* schools.

Here is an instance where we have to pay very close attention to the kinds of disparities or inequalities that are associated with the particular type of instruction and teaching content that takes place within a school. Many people thought that desegregation of schools in the United States would introduce a so-called level playing field in terms of the quality of schooling that is provided to all kids. But, in fact, in many schools in the United States, instruction has been resegregated *within* schools by varying the assignment of kids who are black and white to different levels or qualities of curriculum and instruction in the same school building.

But another issue that I think has emerged in work on education and schooling is the connection to eventual labour market outcomes. Those members of the denigrated group who actually manage to attain higher levels of schooling despite processes that tend to channel them away from academic success will not necessarily face fair treatment in the labour market. We are discovering that as individuals from denigrated groups attain higher and higher levels of education, they may face *rising* discriminatory wage penalties. This appears to be the case for Afro-Americans in the United States and for Afro-Brazilians in Brazil (Tomaskovic-Devey, Thomas and Johnson, 2005; Arias, Yamada and Tejerina 2004). So, although individuals from a denigrated group who acquire higher levels of education from the denigrated group earn more than individuals from their same group with lower levels of attainment, they suffer greater discriminatory penalties vis-à-vis individuals with comparable levels of education from the privileged group. Education does not provide insulation from discrimination. Quite the contrary, it actually can aggravate the degree of discrimination confronting these individuals.

A fourth area of interest to stratification economists has been racial and ethnic disparities in patterns of self-employment or formation and maintenance of small businesses. An argument can be made that ethnic groups that face discrimination in hiring may display higher rates of self-employment as a response to adversity. It would be useful to determine whether higher levels of self-employment among particular ethnic and racial groups are a consequence of the fact that they have less opportunity to be hired for employment by others, or a consequence of the fact, as is frequently assumed by cultural determinists, that a disproportionately higher number of members of that group might have a stronger preference or inclination for entrepreneurship. This merits closer investigation, particularly with respect to the self-employment experience of immigrant communities.

The Effects of Skin Shade Variation

Now let me come to a topic that I am not sure is familiar to many of you, but there is a fifth body of research that has been closely allied to the stratification economics research programme that involves examining the effects of skin shade variation and phenotype variation on labour market outcomes. One of the papers that I did with Art Goldsmith and Darrick Hamilton was based upon the use of the Multi-City Study of Urban Inequality (MCSUI).

MCSUI is a data set in which the interviewers were assigned the responsibility of coding the skin shade of the individual they were interviewing. Interviewers were given a chart to assist them in assigning the individual's skin shade, based on a range from very light to light to medium to dark to very dark. The interviewers' reports on respondents' skin shades permitted us to investigate whether or not colour had any salience in explaining variations in wage outcomes among African Americans males.

It is well established that it is a mistake to treat all immigrant groups as having the same experience, that there is heterogeneity in experiences across immigrant groups. The same argument can be made when looking at members of a specific sub-national group, that there also can be heterogeneity in experience within that group itself.

In the context of the US situation, we found that there were significantly higher wage penalties faced by dark-skinned and medium-skinned black men than for light-skinned black men. In fact, our results demonstrated that light-skinned black men actually face similar labour market conditions, although not identical, to white men (Goldsmith et al., 2007).

We also have explored the relationship between skin shade and opportunities for African American women in the marriage market. We found that lighter-skinned African American women were more likely to marry earlier and to remarry – if the initial marriage did not last – than darker-skinned African American women. The marriage penalty for darker skin shades clearly is not unique to the United States. For example, if one were to visit a country like India you would find that in the marital advertisements that circulate in the newspapers there frequently are specific requests for brides who are 'wheatish' or fair-skinned in complexion. There is also a wide international use of dangerous skin-lightening creams in countries ranging from India to Jamaica to Uganda (Hamilton et al., 2008).

Jennifer Eberhardt, a psychologist at Stanford University, led a research team in conducting a fascinating project to establish whether there is a skin shade and phenotype penalty associated with the way in which people are treated by the criminal justice system. Her team found that for black men convicted of the same type of capital crime in the state of Pennsylvania, those who were lighter skinned and who had features that were 'less' black looking were far less likely to get the death penalty than the black men who were darker skinned and who had features that were 'more' black looking (Eberhardt et al., 2006).

Similar results with respect to employment have been found by Frank et al. (2010) in a paper in the *American Sociological Review*. Their paper focuses on Latinos in the United States and employs the New Immigrant Survey (NIS) collected in 2003. Interviewers used a more detailed skin shade measure – a scale scored from 1 to 10 – from very light to very dark. One of the more intriguing discoveries here that was uncovered by a student of mine, Alexis Rosenblum (2009), is if one was to use the race response in the NIS for Latino respondents, no evidence of discrimination against Latino immigrants will be found. However, if you use the interviewer coded skin shade measure, you will find substantial evidence of discriminatory penalties for darker-skinned Latinos. Why is that the case?

Latino respondents tend, regardless of their complexion, to self-report their race disproportionately as white. Now, since there are no true races – or true race classification – since race is, as is frequently observed, a social construct, I am not going to say that their responses are wrong. I do find it intriguing that in this population it is relatively easy to find someone who is extremely dark-skinned saying that their race is white. Why that occurs is the subject for separate investigation, but that tendency among Latino respondents creates a special problem for researchers searching for the presence of racial discrimination.

Darker-skinned respondents, who may actually face discriminatory deficits, flow into the data set via racial self-selection as persons who will be counted as white. This will lead to depression of estimates of discrimination faced by non-white Latinos when the researcher uses the race measure for demarcation of subgroups of the Latino immigrant population. On the other hand, by using the skin shade measure the researcher will pick up substantial evidence of wage discrimination against Latinos with a darker skin colour. This indicates that the stratification economist must be sensitive to the value of understanding how different communities tend to respond to questions about their race, ethnicity and nationality in making a careful investigation of the presence of discriminatory practices against members of that community.

Discrimination Tests

The Chester Beatty Library at Dublin Castle recently housed a gorgeous exhibition that is the product of ethnographic research on the Sikh community in Ireland. I was really struck by one of the narratives where one of the individuals is quoted as saying, 'With my turban on, I am called Bin Laden; if I shave and take off my turban, I am called a Paki'. That resonated with me because of all of the research in which I have been engaged that focuses on how particular ways of looking are penalised and rewarded in the world in which we live. Certain types of appearance may bear heavy social penalties. This might be an area that it would be valuable to explore in greater depth in the Irish context with respect to the circumstances facing what the Canadians might refer to a 'visible minorities'.

I have always found the rhetoric of 'visible minorities' peculiar because I never have been able to comprehend fully what might be an 'invisible minority'. Nevertheless, there are groups that are marked as visibly distinct from what one might view as the mainstream of most societies, and they may be subjected to discrimination as a consequence. Correspondence tests have a special significance in this context. These are tests for discrimination, where letters – false letters of application – are sent to potential employers. The objective is to make use of the relationship between names and addresses as identifiers for ethnicity, national origin or the race of the individual to see if the employer responds differently based upon that information. Researchers using this technique will send two or more applications to a single employer with names that signal different ethnicities and curriculum vitae of a comparable quality.

I believe that this type of strategy is connected to the skin shade research in the following way: the correspondence test, by providing the employer with this name and address that signals a specific ethnic, national origin or racial identity for the faux applicant, is prompting the employer to visualise the individual who is applying for the job. There is a person being conjured up by the recipient of the letter based upon the name and address of the applicant.

Interestingly enough, the correspondence test can be criticised for limiting our capacity to identify discriminatory behaviour to the point of initial access or application for the job. It cannot give us much information about what might happen subsequently because, in such tests, if the employer responds by saying 'Come for an interview', the researcher will respond via their applicant persona that he or she has taken another job. The 'applicant' never shows up for the interview.

However, there is a new article by Dryadis and Vlassis (2010) published in the *Manchester School* on ethnic discrimination in Greece. They extended the correspondence test by using testers and actors to receive phone calls when the employers seek to arrange interviews. They sought to determine whether there was a divergence in treatment of applicants for jobs in Greece between Greeks and Albanians. Specifically, Dryadis and Vlassis wanted to see whether or not the employer would provide information of the possibility of a wage offer, how much that wage offer might be, and whether or not the employer might offer to register the individual for insurance.

Here is what they found: The probability of getting an interview call – or a call to arrange an interview – was 21.4 per cent lower for Albanians than for Greeks. When calls were made, the potential wage offers were 11 per cent lower against the Albanians. Finally, Albanians were 26 per cent less likely to be offered to be registered for insurance. The correspondence test combined with actors on the phones made it possible to try to gain more information about how much discrimination might occur at subsequent stages of the application process. Ultimately, I would contend that carefully designed and adequately financed audit studies that rely on trained actors to pursue various stages of the employment process are the gold standard for the detection of discrimination in employment.

The sixth and final set of studies that I want to mention involves work that I have done with Major Coleman and Rhonda Sharpe (Coleman et al., 2008). In 2008 we published a paper in the *American Journal of Economics and Sociology*. We tried to address some of the possible limitations of self-reports of discrimination. Once again, we used data from the Multi-City Study of Urban Inequality, exploiting the fact that respondents reported whether or not they had experienced discrimination in the workplace and, specifically, whether they had experienced wage discrimination.

In addition to examining those responses, we used the standard kind of statistical procedures that are customarily used to try to detect discrimination to determine the relationship between each individual's response to whether or not he or she had been subjected to work based discrimination, and separate measures of whether or not they actually had experienced wage discrimination. Hence, we were comparing the self-reported measures against our own independent actual measures of discrimination. We found in this US-based data set that black respondents grossly underestimated the extent to which they had been exposed to discrimination, while white respondents grossly overestimated the extent to which they had been subjected to discrimination. To the extent that researchers utilise self-reports of discrimination in the process of measuring the extent of the phenomenon faced by a group, it will be important to complement the study with ethnographic research that can help indicate the extent to which the group may tend to overreport or underreport its exposure to discrimination.

Conclusion

Patently, the research findings from the programme of investigation pursued under the rubric of stratification economics reveals that there is a blatant misperception by those who suggest that the US has become a post-racial society. To some degree that misperception has been strongly consolidated for many individuals by the election of Barack Obama as President. Furthermore, Obama himself played to those beliefs, especially via the messianic images that he mobilised in his campaign.

At one stage in the campaign he made a distinction between the Moses generation and the Joshua generation. The Moses generation would include the individuals who were founding actors of the civil rights movement in the United States, key figures in the 1960s. Obama then described his own generation as the Joshua generation, the generation that finally reaches the Promised Land. By invoking arrival at the Promised Land, Obama virtually suggested that his own election constituted a symbolic representation of the coming of post-racial America.

I admit that I have never been able to figure out where my own generation lies in Obama's metaphorical scheme; perhaps we are permanently lost in the wilderness? But so be it. Furthermore, throughout much of his conversation on the campaign trail and subsequently, Obama has placed a rhetorical emphasis on personal responsibility and internal correctives within the black community as the solution for ongoing racial disparities in the society. He even expressed a certain sympathy for white hostility towards affirmative action and has made it clear that he will not support race-specific programmes on behalf of blacks in the United States.

As a researcher who explores intergroup disparity, I feel compelled to be honest and careful, even if it means in my case being a black scholar whose findings challenge the narrative that is being utilised by the first openly black President of the United States. I submit that we should be very cautious about even treating this notion of post-raciality as a desirable ideal. We must recognise that wherever we are we should not be seeking a race-blind, caste-blind, ethnicity-blind society per se. What we should be seeking instead is a race-fair, caste-fair, ethnicity-fair society. That desire animates and motivates my personal research programme. I think the notion of fairness, rather than blindness, is central to all thinking today while we address the problem of intergroup inequality and the mechanism of discrimination as a means of perpetuating such inequality.

References

Arias, O., Gustavo Y., and Tejerina, L. (2004), 'Education, Family Background and Racial Earnings Inequality in Brazil' *International Journal of Manpower* 25:3-4, , pp. 355-374.

Coleman, M., Darity, W., and Sharpe, R. (2008), 'Are Reports of Discrimination Valid? Considering the Moral Hazard Effect' *American Journal of Economics and Sociology* 67:2, April, pp. 149-175.

Darity, W. (2005), 'Stratification Economics: The Role of Intergroup Inequality' *Journal of Economics and Finance* 29:2, June, pp. 144-153.

Derbyshire, J. (2009), *We Are Doomed: Reclaiming Conservative Pessimism* New York: Crown Forum.

Dryadis, N. and Vlassis, M. (2010), 'Ethnic Discrimination in the Greek Labour Market: Occupational Access, Insurance Coverage and Wage Offers' *The Manchester School* 78:3, June, pp. 201-218.

Eberhardt, J., Davies, P.G., Purdie-Vaughans, V. and Johnson, S.L. (2006) 'Looking Deathworthy: Perceived Stereotypicality of Black Defendants Predicts Capital-Sentencing Options' *Psychological Science* 17:5, pp. 383-386.

Goldsmith, A., Hamilton, D. and Darity, W. (2007), 'From Dark to Light: Skin Color and Wages Among African-Americans' *Journal of Human Resources* 42:4, Fall, pp. 701-738.

Hamilton, D., Goldsmith, A. and Darity, W. (2009), 'Shedding "Light" on Marriage: The Influence of Skin Shade on Marriage for Black Females' *Journal of Economic Behavior and Organization* 72:1, October, pp. 30-50.

Herrnstein, R. and Murray, C. (1994), *The Bell Curve: Intelligence and Class Structure in American Life* New York: Free Press.

Loury, G. (2002), *The Anatomy of Racial Inequality* Cambridge: Harvard University Press.

Morin, R. (1995), 'A Distorted Image of Minorities: Poll Suggests That What Whites Think They See Might Affect Beliefs', *The Washington Post*, 8 October.

Morin, R. (2001), 'Misperceptions Cloud Whites' View of Blacks' *The Washington Post*, 11 July.

Oliver, M. and Shapiro, T. (1995), *Black Wealth/White Wealth: A New Perspective on Racial Inequality* New York: Routledge,.

Rosenblum, A. (2009), *Looking Through the Shades: The Effect of Skin Color by Region of Birth and Race for Immigrants to the USA*, Sanford School of Public Policy Honors Thesis, Duke University, December

Simon, H. (1976), 'From Substantive to Procedural Rationality' in S.J. Latsos (ed.) *Method and Appraisal in Economics*, Cambridge: Cambridge University Press, pp. 378-401.

Tomaskovic-Devey, D., Thomas, M. and Johnson, K. (2005), 'Race and the Accumulation of Human Capital Across the Career: A Theoretical Model and Fixed Effects Application', *American Journal of Sociology*, 111:1 July, pp. 58-89.

Wax, A. (2009), *Race, Wrongs and Remedies: Group Justice in the 21st Century*, Lanham: Rowman and Littlefield.

Chapter 7

Assessing Unequal Treatment: Gender and Pay[1]

Mary Gregory

The second half of the twentieth century brought a major transformation in the economic and social status of women. In one of the most sustained and striking developments of the era the numbers of women in paid employment expanded at an unprecedented rate throughout the advanced economies, leading, in some countries, to near parity with the numbers of men in the labour force. Across the OECD economies the female share in employment is now 45 per cent, highest in the Nordic nations (over 48 per cent in Finland) and lowest, just over 40 per cent, in southern Europe. This massive expansion in women's labour force participation has halved the gender employment gap. This feminisation of the workforce in numerical terms has been paralleled by qualitative changes as women enter occupations and industries from which they were previously absent, or

[1] This paper draws on work carried out over a number of years in collaboration with Sara Connolly. I am also indebted to colleagues in the Low Wage Employment Network (LoWER) with whom I shared research projects, conferences and discussions. Funding support from the EU for the LoWER Network is gratefully acknowledged, and collaboration in particular with Wiemer Salverda, Miriam Beblo and Ioannis Theodossiou. This review paper draws in particular on Gregory, 2009; Gregory et al., 2009; and Connolly and Gregory, 2008, 2009.

enter these in increasing numbers. This development is particularly marked in managerial positions and the professions. With this progressive shift of women's economic activity from household to market place women's earnings now make an increasingly important contribution to the household's income, enhancing their status and bargaining power within it. These developments have brought women an unprecedented degree of financial independence, and been a key element in the transformation of their economic and social position.

But while women continue to make major strides towards economic equality, the transformation remains seriously incomplete. Equality of outcomes in the labour market has not been achieved. The advanced economies show equalising but still unequal employment between men and women. Women typically receive lower pay; they feature disproportionately among the low-paid; they remain under-represented in prestige professions and 'top jobs'. Unacknowledged in GDP figures women still provide most of the care for children and the elderly, often constraining their labour market participation – the 'double burden'. Women's lower earnings in employment and shorter working lives bring lower lifetime earnings, reduced pension entitlements and a greater risk of poverty in old age. All these factors contribute to the continuing economic inequality of women.

From the many dimensions of inequality and its continually changing profile this chapter focuses on the gender pay gap, and specifically on three areas where new analytical techniques and/or improved data are allowing us not only to develop better measures of the pay gaps but to gain greater insight into the channels through which they arise. This clarification of the channels hopefully will give a firmer basis for the further development of policy. The first area examined focuses on the estimation of the gender pay gap at different points across the earnings distribution. Quantile regression techniques have brought to the fore that the gender pay gap is most pronounced at the top end of the earnings distribution – the 'glass ceiling'. The processes underlying the glass ceiling, through job assignments within the firm, are beginning to be addressed through new types of data: personnel records from within the firm. The following section confronts the core issue of the 'family gap', the pay penalty associated with motherhood. Since family-friendly policies are now at the forefront of the equality agenda establishing best-practice estimates of their effects is an immediate challenge. We report on two recent studies which exemplify contemporary analytical techniques. The third area considered is motivated by the role of part-time employment for women. In a number of EU countries this is a favoured method for women to achieve work-family reconciliation, and its further development has the endorsement of the European Commission, following the Kok report. But part-time jobs are often of poor quality, involving low pay and poor career progression. In this section we report on analyses of the impact of a spell in part-time work on women's subsequent employment and earnings profiles, highlighting the permanent earnings penalty brought about by occupational downgrading on the switch to part-time work. The final section summarises the methodological messages, and briefly assesses the likely drivers of future trends in women's labour market position.

Measuring the Gender Pay Gap: Quantile Regressions and the Glass Ceiling

The gender pay gap is typically seen as the central issue in women's economic inequality. The crudest form of gender discrimination, separate pay rates for men and women are now illegal in all advanced economies, and often for decades already. But the gender pay gap survives universally.

While the detailed pattern varies, the salient features of women's lower pay relative to men are common across countries. As Figure 1 illustrates for three leading economies, the UK,

Germany and the US, women's earnings are below those of men right across the earnings distribution. Women are concentrated at lower pay levels and heavily outnumbered at high earnings. The earnings disadvantage applies across the life-cycle. Even as they enter the labour market women tend to be lower paid; in their late 20s they experience a major loss of ground which persists over the remaining years of their working lives.

Figure 1a: Male and Female Average Earnings, US, 2006

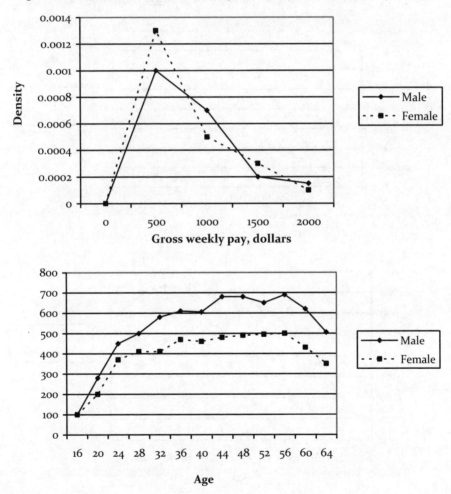

Source: US Current Population Survey. Earnings by age: male earnings at youngest age = 100

To summarise the gender pay gap in a single statistic, a comprehensive analysis by the OECD estimates the unweighted average of women's hourly pay across the OECD countries at 84 per cent of men's, a pay gap of 16 per cent (OECD, 2006). In the US the gap is around 23 per cent, and in EU countries between 10 per cent and 25 per cent; relatively low gaps characterise Belgium, Scandinavia and Eastern Europe; gaps are higher in much

Figure 1b: Male and Female Average Earnings, Germany, 2006

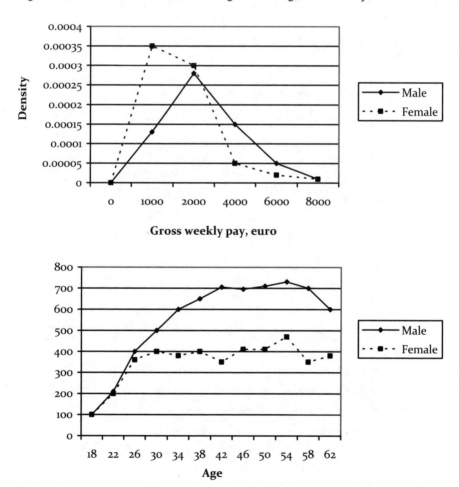

Source: Germany Socio-Economic Panel. Earnings by age: male earnings at youngest age = 100

of Western Europe, notably the UK. Overall, the pay gap is estimated to have narrowed by approximately half since the 1960s, although this progress has recently faltered at both ends of the range, in the low-gap Scandinavian countries and high-gap US (Blau and Kahn, 2006).

Figure 1c: Male and Female Average Earnings, UK, 2006

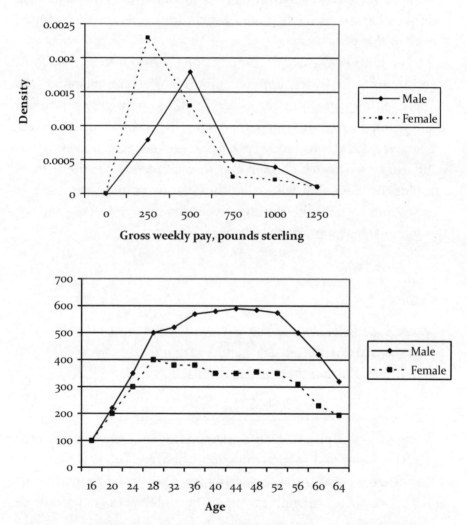

Source: UK Annual Survey of Hours and Earnings. Earnings by age: male earnings at youngest age = 100

Pay gaps make headlines, but are, of course, very poor guides to the presence or otherwise of unequal treatment. Pay differentials reflect differences in individuals' productive characteristics (education, experience, ability and motivation) and in the net advantages, including economic rents, of their workplaces. Discrimination arises only in the part of the pay gap due to unequal rewards for like characteristics, or unequal treatment due to unlike characteristics (gender) which are irrelevant to performance in the job.

The Blinder-Oaxaca decomposition,[2] introduced in the 1970s, continues to be widely applied and gives powerful insights. This approach disaggregates the observed differential between men's and women's pay into the part which reflects differing characteristics relevant to productivity in work, and the part reflecting the differing rewards which men and women receive for these characteristics. Denoting (the logarithm of) men's and women's pay as w_M and w_F, and their productive characteristics as X_M and X_F, pay for each group can be written:

$$w_M = X_M b_M$$

$$w_F = X_F b_F$$

where b_M and b_F denote the pay reward per unit of productive characteristics received by men and women respectively. The gender pay gap can then be decomposed as:

$$w_M - w_F = (X_M - X_F)b_F + X_M(b_M - b_F)$$

where $(X_M - X_F)$ gives the differences in the productive characteristics which men and women bring to the job, and $(b_M - b_F)$ measures the differing rewards to these attributes. The second term, the part of the earnings gap not explained by differences in productive characteristics, is taken as an estimate of discrimination.

---

[2] See Blinder(1973), Oaxaca (1973) and Oaxaca and Ransom (1994).

There is a wide measure of agreement across a multitude of individual country studies and the smaller number of international comparisons[3] that the narrowing of the 'raw' pay gap over recent decades has involved both dimensions. The gap in characteristics has been substantially reduced as rising educational attainment and employment continuity raise women's human capital; among younger cohorts this now at least matches men's, although a gap remains among older cohorts. Estimates of the unexplained pay gap indicate it also has been declining over time. In terms of the OECD estimates cited above, of the 'raw' gap of 16 per cent, differences in characteristics are now of minor importance, while the unexplained component averages 15 per cent of male earnings.[4]

The Blinder-Oaxaca approach has served us well for many years, but the estimation of discrimination as the residual after the 'explained' component implies that any omitted variables or errors of measurement or specification become attributed as discrimination. This continually challenges us to refine the estimates of the 'explained' component. One restriction implied in the Blinder-Oaxaca approach is that each conditioning characteristic has a single unit return (b_M, b_F) which applies across the earnings distribution. Quantile regression relaxes this restriction, by estimating the return to each characteristic specific to different quantiles within the distribution. Not only does this allow greater insight into the ways in which the conditioning variables impact, but these more targeted estimates improve the precision of the 'explained', and therefore the 'unexplained', component of the pay gap.

---

[3] Leading instances include Blau (1998) for the US, Joshi and Paci (1998) for the UK and Clarke (2001) for EU countries; Jarrell and Stanley (2004) and Weichselbaumer and Winter-Ebmer (2005, 2007) report recent meta-analyses.

[4] As an unweighted average across countries the OECD estimates may be a lower bound; alternative estimates, using rather different data and definitions, often come in somewhat higher.

One of the most comprehensive studies applying quantile regression is Arulampalam, Booth and Bryan (2007). Using harmonised data for 11 countries in the pre-enlargement EU available in the European Community Household Panel, they find for each country a positive and statistically significant gender wage gap at all quantiles across the earnings distribution, attributable to the inferior returns women receive for their productivity-generating characteristics. The most striking finding from the study is that the lower returns earned by women, and therefore the gender gap, are most pronounced at the upper end of the distribution – the 'glass ceiling'. Defining a glass ceiling to exist when the wage gap at the 90th percentile is at least two percentage points higher than in any of the lower percentiles they find the presence of a glass ceiling in nine of their eleven countries, and in six countries (including the UK and Germany) that the pay gap is increasing all the way up the distribution. Conversely, they find only slight evidence of a 'sticky floor' in women's pay, a differentially severe wage gap at the bottom of the distribution.[5]

Arulampalam et al. also find that women partially offset these adverse returns by superior characteristics. At the 10th percentile in only five of the eleven countries do women have superior characteristics to men; this rises to seven countries at the 50th percentile, and to nine at the 90th percentile (the exceptions are Denmark and Germany). Only at the bottom of the distribution do men tend to have superior characteristics; over most of the distribution women are on average better qualified than men at comparable quantiles. This superiority in characteristics is, however, insufficient to offset the lower rewards they receive for these characteristics. This disadvantage is particularly strong for women towards the upper end of the earnings distribution.

---

[5] Spain is found to be the exceptional case in distributional aspects, with no glass ceiling and a sticky floor, and a pay gap which decreases up the earnings distribution.

A country not included in the study by Arulampalam et al. but conspicuous for its gender equality, including a low average gender pay gap, is Sweden. There too the raw pay gap increases sharply at the top of the earnings distribution. In their seminal study Albrecht, Bjorkland and Vroman (2003) similarly establish that it is the differential rewards that women receive for their characteristics, not differences in these characteristics, that account for the gender gap at the top of the distribution. In an interesting twist, however, their data allow them also to examine the impact of 107 occupations; they find that controlling for detailed occupation substantially reduces the estimated gender gap at the top of the wage distribution. They argue emphatically, however, that at the top end occupation and pay are jointly determined; controlling for occupation is 'really another way of showing the glass ceiling effect, which manifests itself partly through occupational segregation', and that 'occupational segregation is the form in which the glass ceiling is manifested rather than an independent explanation of it'.

This distributional evidence on the gender wage gap, and particularly the glass ceiling, obtrudes the issue of gender differences in job assignment, including promotions. Establishing gender differences in job assignment and promotions requires a very specific context and suitably detailed data. The best sources, where available, are personnel records within the firm, allowing scrutiny of the working of the internal labour market within the firm, where these decisions are made.[6] An excellent recent instance is the study by Ransom and Oaxaca (2005) of a US regional grocery store chain facing a class-action lawsuit over gender discrimination. This yielded eleven years of personnel data, including job titles, wage rates and earnings, job assignments, transfers and promotions. Modelling worker movements within the firm as a

---

[6] Seminal contributions here are Baker, Gibbs and Holmstrom (1994a,b).

Markov process in transition probabilities across jobs they find a pattern of initial job assignment and intra-firm mobility, including into supervisory and management positions, that generally penalised women. Using regression methods to further control for characteristics (women were on average better qualified than male employees) they found men to be six times more likely to be promoted than women, even after control for characteristics including age and tenure. Most significantly, pay differences were found to be almost completely associated with differences in job assignments between men and women.

Although the data and methodology of the Ransom and Oaxaca study are particularly interesting, the fact that this firm faced a discrimination action suggests that the outcomes there were relatively extreme. Other evidence, however, is not lacking. For example, for the UK Booth et al. (2003) using the British Household Panel Survey find that women derive smaller pay gains from promotion than men. Within the academic profession in the US gender differences in salaries reflect women's lower promotions (Ginther and Hayes, 2003), findings corroborated for economists in UK universities by Blackaby et al. (2005). Even where appointments and promotions are subject to well defined procedures, as typically in large organisations, placings within a specified scale depend on individual negotiation and employer discretion. In this process the evidence indicates disadvantage for women in placing, promotion probabilities and subsequent pay gains.

An insightful addendum to these studies is given by Landers et al. (1996). In a study of two large US legal partnerships they show that criteria for promotion including billable hours can lead to a 'rat race' equilibrium with inefficiently long hours worked. They further note: 'this selection process may have the effect, although not the intent, of keeping a disproportionate number of qualified women out of leadership positions in business and professional organizations.'

Measuring the 'Family Gap': Evidence on Maternity Breaks

As is clear from Figure 1, the emergence of a substantial gender pay gap correlates closely with women's childbearing and child-care years. The 'motherhood penalty' or 'family gap' and its contribution to the gender pay gap, is widely confirmed in studies using microdata. Waldfogel (1998a, 1998b) finds that family status directly explains 40-50 per cent of the gender gap in the US and UK, with a further 30-40 per cent attributable indirectly, through the effect of employment interruptions on human capital; these motherhood effects are clearly a major component of the gender gap.[7]

The scale of this challenge to gender equality is growing. A major force driving female employment growth has been the movement of mothers into paid work outside the home, with employment breaks for child-rearing now fewer and shorter. This increasingly includes mothers with young children; in the US and the UK one out of two new mothers now returns to work before the baby's first birthday. In recognition of the pervasiveness of labor market participation by mothers, the thrust of social policies towards gender equality in most countries now centres on family support, with the reconciliation of work and family a major new focus. One of the major responses is in the extension of maternity leave. Under EU Directives all member states now provide a minimum of 14 weeks of maternity leave, with job protection and, typically, full income replacement. In addition, all countries now provide a further period of job-protected leave, varying from a minimum of three months up to three years, often unpaid, sometimes with partial income replacement. While many countries make this leave formally

---

[7] Similar results are obtained for Australia by Chapman et al. (2001) and by Harkness and Waldfogel (2003) for seven countries, among many others.

transferable between parents, in practice it is overwhelmingly taken by mothers.

Assessing the social efficiency of maternity leave is not straightforward. Supporters claim that by allowing mothers a job-protected break for childcare it obviates potential withdrawal from the labour force and preserves good job-matches, while its statutory basis gives improved status to working mothers. But any employment interruption implies forgone work experience, reducing the accumulation of human capital. Even with job protection separation from the previous employer may result, bringing the further loss of firm-specific human capital.[8] In addition, human capital may depreciate, as skills, or confidence in them, atrophy through lack of use or become obsolete with, for example, developments in software or office technology. These losses will increase with the length of the non-employment spell. Any maternity break, particularly a longer one, may be viewed as a signal of lower work commitment, reducing returns to current characteristics and inhibiting selection into training and career advancement.

We now review the methods and findings of two recent papers which assess the wage implications of motherhood - the 'motherhood pay gap' – in the context of job-protected maternity leave. Both relate to Germany, which offers particularly relevant experience. The duration of leave for childcare is the longest in the EU, up to 36 months beyond the statutory period around the birth, two-thirds of it with income replacement (means-tested), and, importantly, with the right to return to a similarly graded ('status-adequate') job with the previous employer. Although formally transferable between parents, the leave entitlement is virtually universally taken by mothers. Publicly provided childcare is available for only around 9 in 100 chil-

---

[8] Seminal early contributions are by Mincer and Polachek (1974), Corcoran (1977) and Mincer and Ofek (1982).

dren under the age of three, against over 50 in Denmark, and an EU target of 33.[9] This combination of exceptionally generous leave with the scarcity of childcare places gives a strong incentive for German mothers to leave employment and provide an extended period of childcare at home, exposing the tension for mothers between taking advantage of the maternity entitlements and risking their future labour market potential.

Strictly defined, the motherhood pay gap is the difference between mothers' actual earnings and what their earnings would have been had childbearing not occurred. To represent the unobservable counterfactual two methods are now to the fore. The first is based on matching, where individuals in the treatment group (mothers) are paired with a control group of non-mothers, matched as closely as possible on key relevant characteristics. The difference between the earnings of the mothers and the matched group of non-mothers gives the estimate of the motherhood gap. The alternative approach aims to achieve a like-for-like comparison by controlling econometrically for as many sources of variability as possible in the determinants of earnings, including motherhood status. The two papers apply these different techniques.

Beblo et al. (2009) adopt a matching approach, comparing the wages of mothers after return to work with those of otherwise comparable female colleagues who have not taken maternity leave. Using administrative data from the German Institute for Employment Research (IAB), their treatment group is mothers interrupting employment for the birth of a first child and then returning to full-time work in the same establishment, i.e. mothers with strong labour force attachment. Applying propensity score matching based on information two years before the birth they establish two control groups: non-mothers with simi-

---

[9] Family support policies across the EU economies are described in OECD (2007) and Gornick and Meyers (2003).

lar personal characteristics who remain in continuous employment in the same establishment ('monozygotic twin colleagues'), and a much wider control group of non-mothers with
comparable characteristics from all establishments ('dizygotic
twin colleagues'). The double control sample allows investigation of the establishment effect, including how far women in-
tending to have a child may select lower-wage employers (implicitly on the basis of other job advantages). For the monozygotic comparison the motherhood pay penalty one year after the
employment break is estimated as 19 per cent. The main source
of the penalty is that while non-mothers experience continuing
wage growth, mothers not only fail to share in this but experience a small wage reduction on return to the status-adequate
job. The size of the penalty rises with the duration of the employment interruption, exceeding 30 per cent for a three-year
break. Significantly, the penalty is lower for more educated
women, possibly indicating a stronger role for firm-specific human capital in the jobs they hold and the advantage to the employer of restoring the job-match. Dizygotic matching of the
same mothers without firm-specific effects gives an estimated
wage penalty of 26 per cent one year after return, indicating that
mothers tend to select into firms where the wage penalty to interruptions is lower. Since these are women with strong labour
market attachment the authors interpret their estimates as a
lower bound estimate of the motherhood penalty generally.

Buligescu et al. (2009) adopt a wage equation framework and
exploit the richness of the German Socio-Economic Panel
(GSOEP) data to include a comprehensive set of personal, job
and firm characteristics potentially influencing the wage, alongside a detailed specification of the timing and duration of maternity leave taken. A crucial element in the wage equation approach is control for selection into participation. Significant
technical innovations of this paper are the modelling of participation selection as actual hours worked in a tobit specification,

and the use of recently developed estimation techniques to control in this non-linear formulation for sample selectivity, unobserved heterogeneity and the endogeneity of working hours to wages. The authors' preferred estimates give a wage penalty to maternity leave of 10-14 per cent in the first year of return to work. This wage penalty shows an intriguing time profile. For leave taken 2-3 years earlier it becomes virtually non-existent, suggesting swift and full recovery; but it shows a resurgence four years after its commencement, which the authors interpret as an adverse signalling effect involving those mothers who chose to take the maximum leave period available. Tellingly, they find that the wage penalty for employment interruptions for other reasons do not show the same diminishing pattern as maternity leave.

The estimated wage penalties in these two papers differ conceptually but can be matched numerically. The matching approach of Beblo et al. measures the difference in wage outcomes for mothers returning to work against non-mothers. Their estimate of 26 per cent for an average break of 18 months, equivalent to 17 per cent for one year, combines the short-term adverse signalling effect of the employment break with the impact of the forgone work experience. Buligescu et al. measure the impact on the wage of having taken maternity leave, conditional on work experience; the wage cost of a year's lost work experience, around 4 per cent, raises their estimated one-year penalty to 14-18 per cent.

The study by Beblo et al. shows that even 'status-adequate' job protection over a break of up to three years brings a real, as well as relative, earnings loss, a reminder that extended interruptions are likely to reduce productivity, and that employers must be expected to anticipate this. Encouragingly, this earnings setback is estimated to be temporary (Buligescu et al.), consistent with the recovery of productivity and/or revision of employer perceptions. However, the forgone work experience inevitably incurred brings a permanent earnings loss, although with a quadratic experience-earnings profile this penalty will diminish.

Although in the age of 'family-friendly' policies the mother-hood wage penalty remains significant for Germany, under the Scandinavian model the evidence is more encouraging. For Den-mark, where job-protected maternity leave has been mandatory for some years, Datta Gupta and Smith (2002) find that the only adverse effect of children on mothers' earnings is through the loss of work experience; some depreciation of human capital occurs during child-related career interruptions, but the effect is small and temporary. The 'mommy track' appears also not to apply in Sweden; mothers there do not suffer a wage loss for taking paren-tal leave, although household time out of the labor market and unemployment spells carry a wage penalty (Albrecht et al., 1999).

This suggests that where the social climate is supportive of working mothers, as in the Scandinavian countries, the pay pen-alty to maternity leave can be minimal. Where the climate is less supportive, a penalty remains.

Occupational Downgrading in Part-time Work: Revisiting Human Capital

In a number of countries, but not universally, the market has generated its own response to women's wishes to combine work with family in the form of the growth of part-time jobs. The leader by far is the Netherlands, where close to 60 per cent of working women work part-time; the part-time share is close to 40 per cent in the UK and Germany, while in the US, Sweden and Italy it is only around 20 per cent (OECD, 2008). The ex-panded availability of part-time employment opportunities is targeted by the EU as one of the routes through which increased female participation will be achieved.

In Britain, the increase in part-time employment, particularly among women between their mid-20s and early 40s – the peak childcare years – has been a major part of the growth in women's labour market participation which, over successive cohorts, has now fully filled in the dip in the traditional M-shaped age-profile of women's participation.[10] But while women in full-time work have been narrowing the gender pay gap through their rising educational attainment, labour market attachment and occupational diversity, women working part-time have conspicuously failed to match this progress. In 1975 average hourly earnings of women working part-time were 85 per cent of the earnings of women in full-time work, a pay gap of 15 per cent; by the 2000s it was 30 per cent – one of the widest gaps among the advanced economies.[11] This deterioration in their relative position has led to the designation of women working part-time in Britain as 'the new underclass' (Humphries and Rubery, 1995), with the gender pay gap increasingly characterised in terms of 'the part-time pay penalty' (Manning and Petrongolo, 2008). As predominantly engaged in by women, the status of part-time work clearly presents a major issue in gender equality.[12]

Around two-thirds of British women work part-time at some stage of their adult careers, many then returning to full-time work. In addition to the immediate pay gap, therefore, the longer-term impact of a spell in part-time work on subsequent earnings and career trajectories is extremely important. Again, the question presents itself: how far, or on what terms, does part-time work, as a mode of reconciling work and family, support or damage women's labour market position?

---

[10] The elimination of the M-form profile is illustrated in Connolly and Gregory (2007, figure 7.3).

[11] The part-time pay gaps shown in Jaumotte (2003, box 3) give an unweighted average across 13 European countries of 10.5 per cent, and include several countries with a premium.

[12] The requirement of equal treatment in part-time work was secured under the EU's sex discrimination provisions.

Two recent papers, Connolly and Gregory (2008, 2009) identify occupational downgrading as an important concomitant of
the switch to part-time work in Britain, with major adverse implications for future earnings trajectories, even following a return to
full-time employment. A key issue for Connolly and Gregory in
conjunction with pay is the potential underutilisation of women's
skills in part-time work – the 'hidden brain drain' in the words of
the UK's Equal Opportunities Commission. In place of the standard ranking of occupations by average earnings they rank occupations by the average skill level (highest qualification) of those
employed there full-time. Downgrading is then identified by a
move into an occupation where the average skill level is lower.

They find strong evidence of occupational downgrading on
the switch to part-time work. At the level of 15 occupational
groups[13] one-quarter of women moving to part-time work downgrade in occupation. Among the most highly qualified group,
women in the higher professions, the incidence is 20 per cent.
Among associate professionals the rate is similar, 22 per cent,
the majority dispersing to clerical jobs, 17 per cent becoming
carers, and, most seriously, a third moving into the lowest-skill
occupations such as sales assistants. Across professional and associate occupations the average underutilisation of education
due to downgrading is 2.7 years, with substantial patches of
much more severe over-qualification of highly qualified women
working part-time. Managers are notably badly affected.
Twenty-nine per cent of corporate managers downgrade on
switching to part-time work, the majority moving to clerical positions. The most vulnerable group, almost half downgrading,

---

[13] The occupations are: corporate managers; other managers, e.g., in hotels and
retail; teachers; other professionals, e.g., medical practitioners, accountants;
nurses; other associate professionals, e.g., in welfare services; higher clerical jobs;
lower clerical jobs; higher skill services, e.g., police officers, merchandisers; skilled
trades; caring services; other personal services, e.g., chefs, hairdressers; sales assistants; other low-skill jobs, e.g., assemblers, postal workers; cleaners.

are managers of smaller establishments (retail, hairdressing, catering); typically they remain in their line of business but give up their managerial or supervisory responsibilities.[14]

Not all, of course, is bad news. Teaching and nursing are important occupations for women which support part-time employment; 89 per cent of teachers and nurses who switch to part-time work do so while remaining in their professions. Some women, including former managers and professionals, use the switch to part-time work to move into different, still skilled, jobs, indicating career flexibility rather than downgrading.

The incidence of downgrading is only marginally influenced by personal or household characteristics. Having a pre-school child adds only 3-5 percentage points to the 35 per cent risk of downgrading faced by the mother when she leaves her current employer for a new part-time job. What emerges as a major determinant of whether downgrading occurs is the availability of part-time opportunities within her current occupation – where nursing particularly, but also teaching, score well, and corporate management badly. In line with this, across a wide range of occupations the incidence of downgrading is greatly reduced where women cut their working hours while remaining with their current employer.

Connolly and Gregory (2009) build on these findings on occupational downgrading to examine the part-time pay penalty. They show that the wage return to part-time work experience is low – negligible if it is gained in lower-level occupations. This in itself generates a pay penalty to time spent working part-time. However, the major impact on pay comes when the switch to part-time work is accompanied by occupational downgrading and change of employer (which frequently occur jointly). Evalu-

---

[14] Not discussed here are the downgrading experiences of women who take breaks from employment and then return to part-time work. Among them the incidence of downgrading is at least doubled.

ated from the full specification, this combination brings an immediate reduction in hourly earnings of 32 per cent. The switch to part-time work itself, while statistically significant, emerges as economically unimportant. It is the associated occupational downgrading and job change which bring the earnings penalty. The reverse changes, back to full-time work with occupational upgrading into a new job, have symmetric effects, but more muted, with the increase in earnings barely half of the negative impact of the initial switch.

The simulations in Figure 2 show the impact of the switch to part-time work under various scenarios. The baseline case is a woman in a high-skill occupation continuing in full-time work with her current employer. Her earnings follow a consistent upward trajectory as she accumulates high-skill work experience and tenure, gaining 5 per cent in the first year and 65 per cent over ten years. The other three profiles trace the earnings trajectory which results from a switch to part-time work in year 0, followed by five years of part-time work (the sample average), and then a return to full-time work in year 6.

In the first case she downgrades to a low-skill job, while remaining with her current employer. On returning to full-time work she remains in the low-skill occupation with the same employer i.e. the downgrading is permanent. Here the initial earnings setback is around 13 per cent, a loss of 18 per cent against the earnings she would have had remaining full-time in the skilled occupation. Over the six years of part-time work in the low-skill job the earnings trajectory rises only slowly; the immediate impact of the downgrading diminishes, but the return to accumulating part-time low-skill work experience is low. Reverting to full-time work improves the trajectory, but continuing in the low-skill occupation keeps earnings growth depressed below the high-skill trajectory. After 10 years the earnings gap to the base case is around 40 per cent.

Figure 2: Simulated Earnings Profiles with Part-time Work

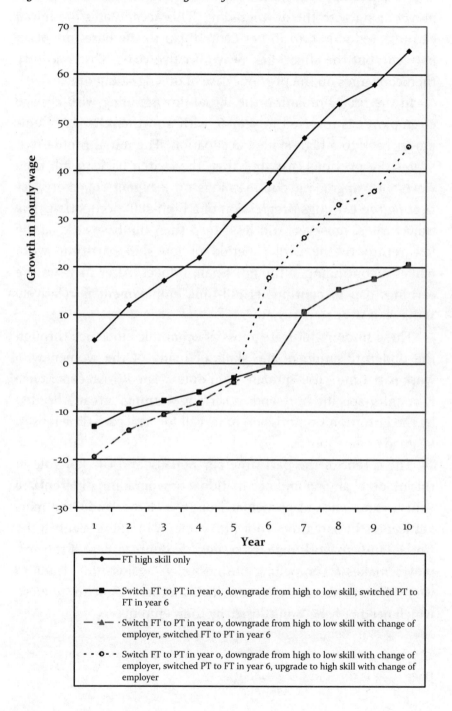

FT high skill only

Switch FT to PT in year 0, downgrade from high to low skill, switched PT to FT in year 6

Switch FT to PT in year 0, downgrade from high to low skill with change of employer, switched FT to PT in year 6

Switch FT to PT in year 0, downgrade from high to low skill with change of employer, switched PT to FT in year 6, upgrade to high skill with change of employer

The next scenario shows the further impact of a change of employer along with the downgrading. This accentuates the initial earnings reduction, to 19 per cent, a gap to the base line of 24 per cent, but the effect dies away over five years. The trajectory then converges on the previous case of downgrading only.

In the final simulation the initial downgrading with change of employer is reversed in year 6, with a further change of employer back to a high-skilled occupation. The initial profile replicates the previous case, but then the switch back to full-time work with upgrading puts earnings on a higher trajectory, reflecting the earnings progression of a high-skill occupation. The trajectory is, however, still less steep than the base case as the low return to the earlier period of low-skill part-time work makes a continuing, although small, impact. After 10 years the earnings gap to continuous full-time employment is relatively stable, but over 20 per cent.

These findings indicate a loss of economic efficiency through the underutilisation of the skills of many of the women who work part-time – the 'hidden brain drain'. The British experience is country-specific but sends a serious warning, already heeded by the European Commission in its call for new part-time jobs to be good quality jobs.

The extent of the part-time pay penalty and the key role in this of job changing and occupational downgrading differentiate British experience in particular from the Netherlands, the market leaders in part-time work in Europe. A mothers' right in the Netherlands to work reduced or flexible hours, except if the employer makes a compelling business case against this, leads to very different outcomes from British mothers' right to 'request' which need only be 'considered' by their employer.

Forward from Here

The methodological implications of the areas reviewed are clear:

- Quantile regression greatly enhances the insights into the channels of the gender pay gap across the earnings distribution

- Personnel records give access to the operation of the internal labour market within firms, job assignments and promotions, where pay differences originate

- The evidence for policy impacts is greatly strengthened by separate studies, using different state-of-the-art techniques and different data

- Occupational downgrading breaks the link between standard measures of human capital and pay

- The channels for the part-time pay penalty need to be identified, and have a lasting impact.

And what of the future?

The 'quiet revolution' in the status of women described by Goldin (2006) seems set to continue. She will define her identity at least in part through her own occupation or career; and her labor force participation decisions will be made autonomously or jointly with a partner, and not as a secondary earner. Two fundamental drivers seem likely to sustain this.

Firstly, the advance of women in education over recent years has been remarkable in both scale and ubiquity. Across the developed economies females now outperform males in educational attainment in most subjects and at most levels. The reasons for this are imperfectly understood, but this development must be expected to underpin rising labour market success for women well into the future.

Secondly, technology continues to bias labour demand in her favour. Shifts in demand patterns are oriented towards services, which often feature the inter-personal 'soft' skills where women have a comparative advantage. Marketisation, the shift to the market of work previously done in the home, mostly by women, is simultaneously creating employment opportunities for women and releasing them from the constraints of home production (Gregory et al., 2007). The demand for skills is rising, at a time when women's gains in educational attainment are qualifying them to meet it. At the same time, women have escaped much of the job destruction affecting male-dominated manual occupations as brain comes to be valued over brawn (Welch, 2000; Weinberg, 2000). This process is characterised by Galor and Weil (1996) as 'female-biased technical change'.

Together these forces will generate continuing pressure for women's advancement in the labour market.

References

Albrecht, J., Bjorklund, A. and Vroman, S. (2003) 'Is There a Glass Ceiling in Sweden?', *Journal of Labor Economics* 21 (1), pp. 145-77.

Albrecht, J.W, Edin, P-A., Sundstrom, M. and Vroman, S.B. (1999) 'Career Interruptions and Subsequent Earnings: A Re-examination Using Swedish Data', *Journal of Human Resources*, 34, 2, pp. 294-311.

Arulampalam, W., Booth, A.L. and Bryan, M.L. (2007) 'Is There a Glass Ceiling over Europe? Exploring the Gender Pay Gap Across the Wage Distribution, *Industrial and Labor Relations Review*, 60 (2) pp. 163-86.

Baker, G., Gibbs, M. and Holmstrom, B. (1994a) 'The Internal Economics of the Firm: Evidence from Personnel Data', *Quarterly Journal of Economics*, 109, 4, pp. 881-919.

Baker, G., Gibbs, M. and Holmstrom, B. (1994b) 'The Wage Policy of a Firm', *Quarterly Journal of Economics*, 109, 4, pp. 921-955.

Beblo, M. Bender, S. and Wolf, E. (2009) 'Establishment-level Wage Effects of Entering Motherhood', *Oxford Economic Papers*, 61, S1, April, pp. 111-134.

Blackaby, D., Booth, A.L. and Frank, J. (2005) 'Outside Offers and the Gender Pay Gap', *Economic Journal*, 115, Feb., pp. F81-107.

Blau, F.D. (1998) 'Trends in the Well-Being of American Women 1970-1995', *Journal of Economic Literature*, XXXVI (1), pp. 113-65.

Blau, Francine D. and Kahn, Lawrence M. (2006) 'The US Gender Pay Gap in the 1990s: Slowing Convergence', *Industrial and Labor Relations Review*, 60, 1, pp. 45-66.

Blinder, A.S. (1973) 'Wage Discrimination: Reduced Form and Structural Estimates', *Journal of Human Resources*, VIII, pp. 436-55.

Booth, A.L., Francesconi, M. and Frank, J. (2003) 'A Sticky Floors Model of Promotions, Pay and Gender', *European Economic Review*, 47, 2, pp. 295-322.

Buligescu, B., de Crombrugghe, D., Menteşoğlu, G. and Montizaan, R. (2009) 'Panel Estimates of the Wage Penalty for Maternal Leave', *Oxford Economic Papers*, 61, S1, April, pp. i35-i55.

Chapman, B., Dunlop, Y., Gray, M., Liu, A., and Mitchell, D. (2001) 'The Impact of Children on Lifetime Earnings of Australian Women: Evidence from the 1990s', *Australian Economic Review*, 34, 4, pp. 373-89.

Clarke, S. (2001) 'Earnings of Men and Women in the EU: the Gap Narrowing but only Slowly', *Statistics in Focus – Population and Social Conditions*, Luxembourg: Eurostat.

Connolly, S. and Gregory, M. (2007). 'Women and Work since 1970', chapter 7 in N.F.R. Crafts, I. Gazeley and A. Newell (eds.) *Work and Pay in Twentieth Century Britain*', pp. 142-77, Oxford: Oxford University Press.

Connolly, S. and Gregory, M. (2008) 'Moving Down: Women's Part-time Work and Occupational Change in Britain 1991-2001', *Economic Journal*, 118, no. 526, February, pp. F52-76.

Connolly, S. and Gregory, M. (2009) 'The Part-time Pay Penalty: Earnings Trajectories of British Women', *Oxford Economic Papers*, 61, S1, April, pp. i76-i97.

Corcoran, M.E. (1977) 'Work Experience, Labor Force Withdrawals, and Women's Wages: Empirical results Using the 1976 Panel of Income Dynamics', in C.B. Lloyd, E.S. Andrews and C.L. Gilroy (eds.) *Women in the Labor Market*', New York: Columbia University Press.

Datta Gupta, N. and Smith, N. (2002) 'Children and Career Interruptions: The Family Gap in Denmark', *Economica*, 69, 4, pp. 609-29.

Galor, O. and Weil, D.N. (1996) 'The Gender Gap, Fertility and Growth', *American Economic Review*, 86, pp. 374-87.

Ginther, D.K. and Hayes, K.H. (2003) 'Gender Differences in Salary and Promotion for Faculty in the Humanities 1977-95', *Journal of Human Resources*, 38, 1, pp. 34-73.

Goldin, C. (2006) 'The Quiet Revolution that Transformed Women's Employment, Education and Family', *American Economic Review*, 96 (2), pp. 1-21.

Gregory, M. (2009) 'Gender and Economic Inequality', in W. Salverda, B. Nolan and T.M. Smeeding (eds.) *The Oxford Handbook of Economic Inequality*, Oxford: Oxford University Press.

Gregory, M., Beblo, M., Salverda, W. and Theodossiou, I. (2009) 'Women and Wages: Introduction', *Oxford Economic Papers*, Special Issue, Vol. 61 No. S1, pp. i1-i10, April.

Gregory, M., Salverda, W. and Schettkat, R. (2007) *Services and Employment: Explaining the US-European Gap*, Princeton, NJ: Princeton University Press.

Harkness, S.E. and Waldfogel, J. (2003) 'The Family Gap in Pay: Evidence from Seven Industrialised Countries, *Research in Labor Economics*, Vol. 22, pp. 369-414.

Humphries, J. and Rubery, J. (eds.) (1995) *The Economics of Equal Opportunities*, London: Equal Opportunities Commission.

Jarrell, S.B. and Stanley, T.D. (2004) 'Declining Bias and Gender Wage Discrimination? A Meta-Regression Analysis', *Journal of Human Resources*, XXXIX (3), pp. 827-38.

Jaumotte, F. (2003) 'Labour Force Participation of Women: Empirical Evidence on the Role of Policy and Other Determinants in OECD Countries', *OECD Economic Studies*, no. 37, OECD, Paris.

Joshi, H. and Paci, P. (1998) *Unequal Pay for Women and Men: Evidence from the British Birth Cohort Studies*, Cambridge MA and London: MIT Press.

Landers, R.M., Rebitzer, J.B. and Taylor, L.J. (1996) 'Rat Race Redux: Adverse Selection in the Determination of Work Hours in Law Firms', *American Economic Review*, 86, 3, pp. 329-48.

Manning, A. and Petrongolo, B. (2008) 'The Part-time Pay Penalty for Women in Britain', *Economic Journal*, Vol. 118, No. 526, February, pp. F28-51.

Mincer, J. and Ofek, H. (1982) 'Interrupted Work Careers: Depreciation and Restoration of Human Capital', *Journal of Human Resources*, 17, Winter, pp. 3-24.

Mincer, J. and Polachek, S. (1974) 'Family Investments in Human Capital: Earnings of Women', *Journal of Political Economy*, 82, Supplement, pp. S76-110.

Oaxaca, R. (1973) 'Male-Female Wage Differentials in Urban Labor Markets', *International Economic Review*, 14 (3), pp. 693-709.

Oaxaca, R. and Ransom, M. (1994) 'On Discrimination and the Decomposition of Wage Differentials, *Journal of Econometrics*, 61, pp. 5-21.

OECD (2006) *Women and Men in OECD Countries*, Paris: OECD.

OECD (2008) *Employment Outlook 2008*, Paris: OECD.

Ransom, M. and Oaxaca, R. (2005) 'Intrafirm Mobility and Sex Differences in Pay', *Industrial and Labor Relations Review*, 58, 2, pp. 219-37.

Waldfogel, J. (1998a) 'The Family Gap for Young Women in the US and Britain: Can Maternity Leave Make a Difference?', *Journal of Labor Economics*, 16, 3, pp. 505-45.

Waldfogel, J. (1998b) 'Understanding the 'Family Gap' in Pay for Women with Children', *Journal of Economic Perspectives*, 12, 1, pp. 137-56.

Weichselbaumer, D. and Winter-Ebmer, R. (2005) 'A Meta-Analysis of the International Gender Wage Gap', *Journal of Economic Surveys*, 19 (3) pp. 479-511.

Weichselbaumer, D. and Winter-Ebmer, R. (2007) 'International Gender Wage Gaps', *Economic Policy*, April, pp. 237-87.

Weinberg, B.A. (2000) 'Computer Use and the Demand for Female Workers', *Industrial and Labor Relations Review*, 53, 2, pp. 290-308.

Welch, F. (2000) 'Growth in Women's Relative Wages and in Inequality among Men: One Phenomenon or Two?', *American Economic Review*, 90, 2, pp. 444-49.

Chapter 8

Disability and Social Inclusion in Ireland[1]

Brenda Gannon and Brian Nolan

In recent years there has been a major shift in the assumptions held about the nature of disability, away from what has been termed the medical model of disability towards what has been termed a social model. The medical model of disability focuses on people's specific impairments, the underlying assumption being that people with a disability are different from the norm and need to be helped and if possible cured so that they might conform to that norm. Starting from the early 1970s, this way of thinking was increasingly challenged and rejected by people with a disability, in favour of what has been termed the social model of disability. The central shift in thinking was that disablement arose from the environment and organisation of society rather than from the individual and their impairment. Disability is seen as a consequence of social, attitudinal and environmental barriers that prevent people from participating in society. The focus is then on the need to change societal conditions to accommodate the needs of the disabled person:

[1] Comments on drafts of the studies summarised here helped to improve them significantly, and we are particularly indebted to Laurence Bond (Equality Authority) in that regard.

those with disabilities should be able to participate in such activities as education, employment and leisure along with everyone else.

This is entirely in tune with the broader focus that emerged over the same period on social inclusion, taken to mean being in a position to participate fully in the life of the society one lives in, while conversely social exclusion entails being prevented from doing so. People with disabilities face many barriers to full participation, and are thus likely to face a heightened risk of social exclusion across various dimensions. The aim of the research studies summarised here, which we carried out for the Equality Authority and the National Disability Authority, was to examine various aspects of inclusion and exclusion for people with disabilities, using available data from representative household surveys of the Irish population. This allowed us to investigate the extent of social exclusion for people with disabilities under the following headings: Education, Labour Force Participation, Earnings, Poverty and Deprivation, and Social Life and Social Participation. In this chapter we outline the thrust of these studies and their key findings, with the reports themselves and associated academic papers containing the full details.[2]

The Data

The main data source used in these studies was the Living in Ireland Survey carried out by the Economic and Social Research Institute from 1994 to 2001, while a special module on disability included with the CSO's Quarterly National Household Survey in 2002 was also used. The measurement of disability in such general household surveys poses considerable definitional and methodological difficulties. In the surveys in question, adults

---

[2] The studies themselves were published as Gannon and Nolan (2004, 2005, 2006), with related papers Gannon and Nolan (2004b, 2007).

reporting chronic or longstanding illness or disability in the surveys can be distinguished, and there is some additional information about the nature of the condition involved and how much it limits or hampers the person. This is fairly crude and cannot serve as substitute for the in-depth information on disability prevalence that has subsequently been obtained via Ireland's National Disability Survey (CSO, 2008, 2010). However, it did allow us to analyse the relationships between the presence of disability and core aspects of societal participation, and thus add substantially to knowledge about disability and social inclusion in Ireland.

In all, about 20 per cent of adults in the Living in Ireland Surveys in a particular year responded that they had a chronic illness or disability. About one-quarter of these said they were not restricted at all in their daily life as a result, while about 55 per cent were restricted to some extent and one-fifth were severely restricted – a distinction that proved particularly valuable in the studies, as we shall see. As expected, reporting disability was strongly linked to age, with only about 13 per cent of those aged 25-34 versus almost half of those aged 65 or over saying they had a chronic illness or disability.

The fact that the Living in Ireland Surveys tracked the same individuals from 1995 to 2001, rather than interviewing a new sample each year, made it particularly valuable in seeking to estimate the impact of disability on people's lives. First, it allowed us to look at the overall experience of disability over a number of years rather than simply the numbers affected at a point in time. This revealed that about twice as many reported such an illness or disability at some point over the seven years as in any one year. We were then able to focus in particular on those reporting persistent illness/disability over all seven years of the panel survey, for whom a particularly pronounced impact might be expected. A total of 180 cases had that experience, accounting for 7 per cent of all respondents and 16 per cent of those who reported disability at any point over the life of the survey. Those experiencing persistent disability were disproportionately older and less well educated than others.

Secondly, the availability of information on the same individuals over time meant that, for some, the onset of disability was captured by the longitudinal survey. This is particularly valuable in trying to pin down the impact of disability on the various socio-economic outcomes of interest. On almost all the measures studied, people with chronic illness or disability fared worse than others in their own age group. It is however difficult to tease out from a 'snap-shot' at a single point in time the precise role played by disability itself, as opposed to other factors – since those affected by disability may also be distinctive in other ways, including in terms of characteristics that may affect outcomes but are not measured in the survey (such as ability, motivation and attitudes). The Living in Ireland Surveys followed the same people from one year to the next, and so can be used to track individuals not experiencing disability and then subsequently reporting disability, and others who move from reporting disability to not doing so. The change in the outcomes of interest – labour force status, earnings, household income and social participation – as disability status changes can then be studied directly. This improves our capacity to estimate the effects of disability with precision and allows the channels whereby these effects operate to be traced with more confidence. The impact of disability 'onset' was studied by focusing on persons in the survey who reported no chronic illness or disability for two years, followed by two years when they do report illness or disability. They were compared with those 'at risk' of onset who did not actually experience it – in other words, those who reported two consecutive years without disability in the panel and were then observed for a further two years without disability.

Disability and Education

In assessing the impact of disability on key socio-economic outcomes we start with education. The relationship between disability and educational attainment is a complex one: disability may have a negative impact on educational attainment, but low education is also associated with an enhanced risk of becoming disabled. One can first simply compare levels of educational attainment for adults reporting chronic illness or disability in the 2001 Living in Ireland Survey with other adults. Half those who were ill or disabled had no formal educational qualification, compared with one-fifth of other adults. This partly reflected age, since those with a chronic illness or disability are more concentrated in older ages where educational levels are lowest. However, within each age range the proportion with no educational qualification beyond primary was still much higher for those with long-term disability or illness, and they were also much less likely to have a third-level qualification.

Econometric analysis of the relationship between long-term illness or disability and educational attainment confirmed that, having taken age and gender into account, those reporting a chronic illness or disability that hampered them severely or to some extent were much more likely to have no educational qualifications than those with no illness or disability. This is illustrated in Figure 1, which shows the estimated probability of having no educational qualifications was over 20 percentage points higher for someone with a severely hampering disability. It also shows that those individuals were less likely to have third level education. On the other hand, those with an illness or disability that does not hamper them in their daily activities were statistically indistinguishable from those with no illness or disability.

It is then useful to distinguish between those who had the illness or disability they were reporting in the survey from before the age of 25 – when an impact on educational attainment might be expected – and those only affected after 25, when such a direct impact would be unlikely. Illness or disability present before 25 and where the respondents were hampered in their daily lives was indeed associated with a substantially increased likelihood of having no qualifications and a reduced chance of having a third-level qualification. However, illness or disability that only affected the person after age 25, where the individuals were hampered in their daily lives, was also estimated to have a negative (though more modest) impact.

Figure 1: Disability and Educational Attainment

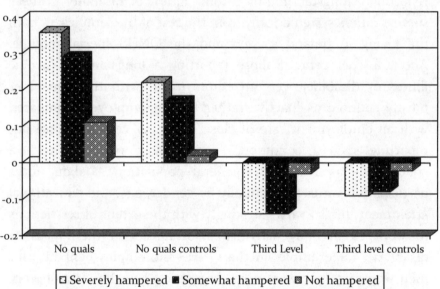

This is probably because the chances of being affected by disability or illness later in life are related to a range of background individual and household disadvantages that increase the likelihood of low levels of educational attainment, and the disability measures are picking up their effects. This might well also be the case to some extent for those affected by illness or disability from before age 25, of course, and means that the scale of the underlying effect of illness or disability *per se* may not be as great as the raw estimates suggest. Even taking this into account, however, disabilities acquired early in life seem to have substantial direct effects on educational attainment. A similar pattern of results was found when analysing data from the special module on disability included with the QNHS in 2002, which had a much larger sample than the Living in Ireland Survey though confined to those of working age.

Disability and Labour Force Participation

Participation in the labour market is for many a central aspect of broader societal participation. The labour market status of those reporting a longstanding or chronic illness or disability in these surveys differs systematically from the rest of the samples, in both the Living in Ireland surveys and the QNHS special module. About 40 per cent of those reporting a longstanding/chronic illness or disability were in employment, with the remainder mostly counted as inactive rather than unemployed, compared with an employment rate of close to 70 per cent for those not reporting such a condition. Among those reporting such a condition – as among the general population – labour force participation varies substantially by gender, age, and educational attainment. It also varies strikingly with the extent of restrictions in work or in daily activities associated with the illness or disability. For example, in the QNHS the employment rate for men who said they were severely restricted in the kind of work they could do was only 18 per cent, and for women in that situation it was only 15 per cent. In the Living in Ireland survey, the employment rate for those who said they were severely hampered in their daily activities by a chronic illness or disability was only 24 per cent, compared with 64 per cent for those who were not hampered.

To disentangle these inter-relationships systematically, we applied regression techniques to identify the influence of the presence of chronic illness or disability, and the extent to which it hampers or restricts the individual, on labour force participation. The results showed that those reporting a longstanding/chronic illness or disability which hampers them in their daily activities or restricts the kind of work they can do have a significantly reduced probability of labour force participation. For men who report being severely hampered or restricted (Figure 2), that reduction is as much as 60 percentage points or more. (For women the corresponding figure is about 50 percentage points.) For those who report being hampered or restricted 'to some extent' rather than severely the effect is much smaller but still substantial. On the other hand, for men reporting a longstanding/chronic illness or disability which did not hamper or restrict them, the probability of being in the labour force was similar to others of the same age, gender and educational attainment and not report any such condition.

The unique longitudinal data obtained in the Living in Ireland survey, which tracked a set of individuals from 1994 to 2000, was also used to look at disability and labour force participation over time rather than in a single snap-shot. While almost 70 per cent of working-age adults in that panel did not report a chronic illness or disability in any year, 6 per cent reported such a condition in every year, and two-fifths of those reporting a chronic illness or disability in the first survey year went on to do so in all six years. There was a stark difference in labour force participation between such people and those not reporting chronic illness or disability. Those reporting such a condition consistently throughout the panel spent an average of only 1.6 years in work over the period, whereas those who never reported such an illness or disability spent 3.5 of the years in work on average. When a range of other personal and household characteristics was taken into account, such persistent disability was estimated to be associated with a 42 percentage point reduction in the likelihood of being in employment. This represents a very substantial reduction, with all the implications that has both for income and for broader participation in the life of society.

Figure 2: Disability and Labour Force Participation: Men

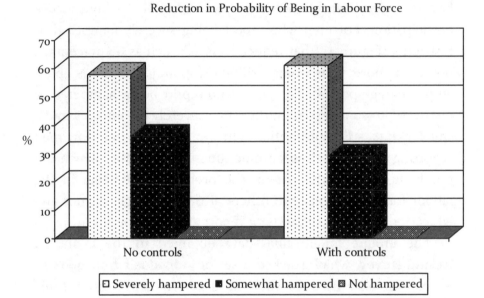

Reduction in Probability of Being in Labour Force

☐ Severely hampered ■ Somewhat hampered ⊞ Not hampered

Tracking individuals from before the onset of disability through the period of onset and beyond, a substantial and sustained decline in their employment rate was also seen. As Figure 3 shows, only about 60 per cent of these individuals were in employment prior to onset – they were already more prone to unemployment and inactivity than others. When disability onset then occurred the employment rate for these individuals fell from 60 per cent to 46 per cent, and in the year after onset this fell a little more to 43 per cent. Statistical analysis of these individuals showed that, having taken a range of personal and household characteristics into account, the onset of disability which did not hamper the person in their daily activities was associated with a decline of about 10 percentage points in the probability of being in employment, whereas when it did hamper them that reduction was close to 30 percentage points.

Figure 3: Disability Onset and Labour Force Participation

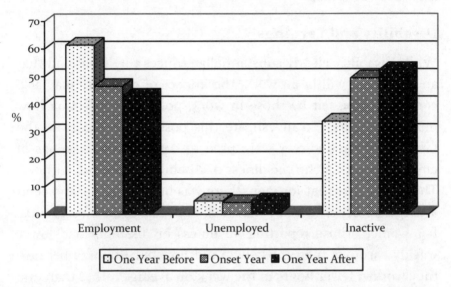

Some comparative perspective on the findings for Ireland can be seen from data for EU countries from the European Community Household Panel survey (of which the Living in Ireland Survey was the Irish element), which asked the same set of questions about longstanding illness or disability in each country. However, the results showed a very wide variation across countries in the percentage reporting a chronic illness or disability, giving rise to severe doubts about whether the responses were capturing the same underlying phenomenon. None the less, it was interesting that the overall employment rate of about 40 per cent for those reporting a chronic illness or disability in Ireland is similar to Belgium and higher than most of the Southern European countries, though lower than Denmark, the Netherlands, and Sweden. Like Ireland, inactivity rather than unemployment accounts for most of the remainder in most of the other countries. Consistently across countries, as in Ireland, there was a substantial differential in employment rate between those reporting that their chronic illness or disability hampered them severely versus 'to some extent' in their daily activities.

Disability and Earnings

While disability clearly substantially reduces the likelihood that an individual will be in work, the impact of disability may also continue to be felt by those in work, potentially affecting how much they earn. To investigate this possibility, data from the Living in Ireland survey were used to compare the earnings of employees with a chronic illness or disability and those without. This found first that for men, there was little or no difference in average hourly or weekly earnings between these two groups. For women, those reporting an illness or disability had lower weekly earnings than those who did not, but this was because they worked fewer hours in the week on average rather than due to lower hourly earnings.

Those with versus those without a chronic illness or disability also differ in terms of other characteristics that would be expected to affect their earnings – notably in terms of age, education and experience. Statistical analysis taking this into account was carried out for men only, since it requires a large number of observations and there are more male employees. When regression analysis was used to 'control' for other factors such as age and experience, the initial results suggested that there was no difference in hourly earnings between those with and those without a chronic illness or disability.

However, those with an illness or disability actually in employment are a minority and may be more likely than average to have characteristics that are not measured or included in the analysis that might positively affect their earnings, such as greater ability or determination. When this is taken into account by a statistical procedure aimed at correcting for such 'sample selection bias', the results did then suggest an earnings gap between those with and without a hampering illness or disability. The extent to which this reflects discrimination *per se* rather than genuine differences in productivity would be very difficult to assess even with much more in-depth information on the individuals and their jobs than was actually available.

This analysis refers to differences in earnings between individuals with the same level of education and previous experience in the workforce; it must be emphasised that illness or disability also has an indirect impact on earnings via its effects on the level of education attained and on years of experience.

Disability and Poverty

Whereas education, labour force participation and earnings vary across individuals, poverty is generally assessed at the level of the household, assuming that the people living in a given household share their resources and have a similar standard of living. In analysing the relationship between disability and poverty we focused on three indicators of poverty used in recent Irish studies. The first looks at whether the income of the household falls below 60 per cent of median income, which is now termed in the EU Social Inclusion process as being 'at risk of poverty'. The second measures enforced basic deprivation, that is going without basic items like proper meals for lack of money. The third indicator measures 'consistent poverty', that is whether someone is both below a relative income threshold and experiencing enforced basic deprivation.[3]

---

[3] For description and discussion of these poverty measures see for example Whelan et al. (2006).

About 38 per cent of adults reporting chronic illness or disability in the 2001 Living in Ireland Survey were found to be at risk of poverty; this was more than twice the rate for other adults. Their consistent poverty rate was over 7 per cent, again about twice the figure for those not reporting a chronic illness or disability. There was a pronounced relationship between degree of reported hampering in daily activities and poverty. Almost half those reporting a chronic illness or disability that severely hampered them in their daily activities were at risk of poverty, and about 16 per cent were in consistent poverty. Where the chronic illness or disability hampered the person to some extent, their consistent poverty rate was a good deal lower, but still about twice that for those with no chronic illness or disability. On the other hand, those with an illness or disability that did not hamper them at all had the same rates of poverty as persons not reporting illness or disability.

Statistical analysis of the relationship between chronic illness or disability and poverty, controlling for other characteristics, identified lower and upper bounds for the estimated impact, reflecting whether educational attainment and current employment – which are both influenced by illness or disability – were controlled for in the models. This analysis suggested that the predicted risk of poverty was between 11 and 22 percentage points higher where the individual had a severely hampering chronic illness or disability, and between 5 and 12 percentage points higher where he or she was hampered to some extent. In terms of consistent poverty, a severely hampering illness or disability was associated with a poverty incidence between 6 and 13 percentage points higher, while an illness or disability that hampered to some extent had a predicted rate 2-4 percentage points higher. Overall, when other influences such as age were accounted for, people hampered severely by their illness or disability had a consistent poverty rate which was five times that of people with no illness or disability.

The number of persons in the household at work and the extent of social welfare dependence were found to play a crucial, interlinked role in determining poverty risk. For ill or disabled persons under 65 years of age, being at risk of poverty was generally associated with there being no one in the household at work. For those aged 65 or over, the number at work in the household was less important but still had a role to play. The other side of the same coin was dependence on social welfare payments: among those with a long-term illness or disability and in households below the 60 per cent of median income threshold (the 'at risk of poverty' threshold), only 10 per cent of household income came from work and most of the rest came from social welfare payments.

Disability onset was seen to be associated with a very substantial increase in the probability of being below that income threshold. Personal and household characteristics of those affected played some role in increasing this risk, but even when they were taken into account disability onset per se increased the 'at risk of poverty' rate by 7 percentage points. Much of this increase in poverty risk was attributable to lower employment. Persistent disability over the life of the panel survey was also strongly linked to lower household income. Even when the personal and household characteristics, including education level, of the individual were taken into account, the predicted household income of someone reporting persistent disability was 20 per cent lower than someone who was otherwise similar but had no experience of disability over the period. Persistent chronic illness or disability thus substantially increased the probability of being below the relative income poverty threshold. When other individual and household characteristics were taken into account, the predicted 'at risk of poverty' rate was 13 percentage points higher for someone who experienced persistent disability, compared with those who experienced no disability over the panel period. Once again reduced employment seemed to be the key channel through which disability increased poverty risk.

Disability and Social Participation

The impact of chronic illness or disability on broader aspects of participation in the life of the community was also explored using information on that topic obtained in the Living in Ireland Survey. The available indicators covered whether the respondent was a member of a club or organisation, how often they talked to neighbours, how often they met friends or relatives (living outside the household), whether they had an afternoon or evening out in the last fortnight that cost money, and whether they intended to vote in the next general election.

Analysis of these responses showed that those with a chronic illness or disability that hampered them severely in their daily activities were much less likely than others to be a member of a club or association, to talk to their neighbours most days, to meet friends or relatives most days, or to have had an afternoon or evening out for entertainment in the last fortnight, and also slightly less likely to say they would vote in a general election. For those with a chronic illness or disability that hampered them only 'to some extent' the picture was more mixed: they had a below-average membership in clubs/associations and were also less likely than average to have had an afternoon or evening out in the last fortnight, but in terms of frequency of contact with neighbours, relatives or friends and voting intentions looked little different to those with no illness or disability. Those with chronic illness or disability that did not hamper them at all were indistinguishable from those with no chronic illness or disability on these indicators.

Regression models were estimated in order to control for differences between the groups being compared in terms of, for example, age and gender, which could affect their levels of social participation. (The measure of intention to vote was omitted at this stage). The results showed that having controlled for those other characteristics, the presence of a severely hampering chronic illness or disability significantly reduced the probability of participation in terms of club membership, frequency of contact with neighbours and with friends or relatives, and having an evening out. The presence of an illness or disability that hampered the individual to some extent was now seen to also be associated with a reduced level of participation on all of the indicators, although the scale of the estimated impact was a good deal less than for severely hampering illness or disability. Individuals reporting chronic illness or disability that did not affect them in their daily activities had predicted participation similar to someone without an illness or disability.

Having a chronic illness or disability throughout the life of the panel significantly affected the expected level of social participation. After controlling for personal and household characteristics, the predicted rate of participation (in all four aspects measured) for those reporting disability throughout the panel was 9 percentage points lower than for those with no experience of disability over the period.

Conclusions

People with disabilities face many barriers to full participation in Irish society. The research summarised here looked at key aspects of participation – education, earnings, poverty and social life – to identify how the experience of people with a long-term disability or illness differs from that of other people. It showed that on almost all the measures studied, people with chronic illness or disability fared significantly worse than others in their own age group. The nature of this disadvantage and the processes which underpin it are extremely complex, and the role of overt discrimination, as opposed to other factors, is particularly difficult to identify. The design of policies to address the barriers to, for example, increased levels of employment is challenging, particularly in the current economic climate. None the less, the experience of other countries shows that the disadvantage associated with disability can indeed be reduced, given the required social investment and attitudinal change.

References

Central Statistics Office (2008), *National Disability Survey 2006 – First Results*, Dublin: Stationery Office.

Central Statistics Office (2008), *National Disability Survey 2006 Volume 2*, Dublin: Stationery Office.

Gannon, B. and Nolan, B. (2004), *Disability and Labour Market Participation*, Dublin: The Equality Authority.

Gannon, B. and Nolan, B. (2004b), 'Disability and Labour Force Participation in Ireland', *Economic and Social Review*, 35 (2), 135-155.

Gannon, B. and Nolan, B. (2005), *Disability and Social Inclusion in Ireland*, Dublin: The Equality Authority and the National Disability Authority.

Gannon, B. and Nolan, B. (2006), *The Dynamics of Disability and Social Inclusion in Ireland*, Dublin: The Equality Authority and the National Disability Authority.

Gannon, B. and Nolan, B. (2007), 'The impact of disability transitions on social inclusion', *Social Science and Medicine*, 64, 1425-1437.

Whelan, C.T., Nolan, B. and Maitre, B. (2006), *Reconfiguring the Measurement of Deprivation and Consistent Poverty in Ireland*, with, Policy Research Series Paper No. 58, Dublin: The Economic and Social Research Institute.

Chapter 9

Multiple Disadvantage: Evidence on Gender and Disability from the 2006 Census

Dorothy Watson and Peter D. Lunn[1]

Introduction

The term 'multiple disadvantage' is used in a number of different senses. Sometimes it refers to the experience of multiple different types of negative outcomes (e.g. Whelan et al., 2001). In other contexts, it refers to the presence of multiple, relatively independent risk factors (Nolan and Whelan, 2009; Berthoud, 2003; Whelan and Maître, 2007). It is in the latter sense that multiple disadvantage is used in this paper.

A common question regarding multiple disadvantage is whether membership in two groups, both of which are disadvantaged in certain respects, is in some sense worse than membership in either one. Barrett and McCarthy (2007), for instance, find that immigrant women in Ireland suffer an additional pay penalty, compared to men and native women. Other research has also shown interactions between life events and social class

[1] We are grateful to the Central Statistics Office for granting access under a pilot scheme to the *Census Research Microdata File (CRMF)* for the project on which this paper is based, and to Helen Russell, Emma Quinn and Chris Whelan for comments on earlier drafts of this paper.

position in accounting for poverty (Vandecasteele, 2005, 2007; Whelan and Maitre, 2008; Lorentzen et al., 2009).

In the present paper, we are looking at the consequences of membership of two relatively independent groups: based on gender and having a disability. The question we ask is whether membership of both groups results in greater disadvantage and, if yes, what form this greater disadvantage takes, and whether the pattern differs across outcomes. We use data from the 2006 Census Research Microdata File to examine the patterns for four outcomes: low levels of education, being outside the labour market, unemployment and being in the unskilled or semi-skilled manual social class.

The concept of multiple disadvantage used here is different from the concept of cumulative disadvantage, which has been used to refer to processes that operate over time, with earlier disadvantage persisting or even interacting with later events to exacerbate disadvantage (e.g. Nolan and Whelan, 1999; Layte and Whelan, 2002; Vandecasteele, 2010).[2] However, by examining several outcome measures, we are able to examine whether risks cumulate across education, labour market participation and unemployment. In other words, are less favourable labour market outcomes accounted for by earlier differences in education, or do people with disabilities face further barriers to participation in the labour market?

Methods

The analysis is based on two sets of hierarchical logistic regression equations run on adults age 25-44 from the 2006 *Census Research Microdata File* (CRMF), access to which was kindly

---

[2] Nolan and Whelan (1999. pp. 9-10) emphasise three elements of the concept of cumulative disadvantage: (a) that a causal sequence over time is involved, (b) that earlier effects persist, and (c) that the impact of earlier factors interacts with later ones (such as, perhaps, a lower return to education for those from deprived backgrounds) (see also Layte and Whelan, 2002; Vandecasteele, 2010).

granted as part of a pilot scheme by the Central Statistics Office for the purpose of the project on which this paper is based. The first set of equations examined the main effects of gender and disability on the four outcomes. This allows us to estimate the independent (net) effects of these factors when other relevant risk factors are controlled. The other factors controlled in the models are family and marital status, religion, ethnicity, nationality, migration, five-year age group, urban/rural location and region. In the models for being outside the labour market, unemployment and social class, education is controlled.[3]

The second set of equations included an interaction term for being a woman and having a disability. This allows us to identify the differences in impact of disability for men and women by comparing the expected risk under two conditions: constraining the impact of disability to be the same for men and women (no interaction) and allowing the impact of disability to differ for men and women (interaction).

A number of patterns are possible, as described by Berthoud (2003) and illustrated in Figure 1. The distinction is based on the main and interaction effects of group membership. *Exponential disadvantage* would arise where membership in both groups, each of which experiences an increased risk of negative outcomes, results in a higher risk than we would expect from the sum of membership in each one. For example, women and people with a disability are less likely to participate in the labour market. If we found that having a disability had a bigger impact on women's labour market participation than on men's, this would be an example of exponential disadvantage.

---

[3] The paper is part of a larger piece of research which uses Census data to elucidate patterns of disadvantage associated with membership in different groups, many of which are small in size. The full models are presented in the main report on this project (see Watson et al, forthcoming).

Figure 1: Illustration of Different Patterns of Multiple Disadvantage

Interaction Effects	Main Effect Present, Positive for Both Groups (++)
Present, positive (+)	**Exponential** (+++): Membership in each group associated with increased risk of negative outcome; membership in both groups associated with *higher* risk than the sum of membership in each.
Not present (o)	**Additive** (++o): Membership in each group associated with increased risk of negative outcome; membership in both groups associated with risk *equal* to the sum of membership in each.
Present, negative (–)	**Non-additive** (++–): Membership in each group associated with increased risk of negative outcome; membership in both groups associated with risk *less* than the sum of membership in each.

A second possibility is *additive disadvantage* (Berthoud, 2003). In this case the risk of negative outcomes is increased but is not intensified by membership of both groups. If we found that having disability reduces labour market participation by the same amount for men and women, this would be an example of additive disadvantage. In this scenario, the impact of having a disability affects men and women equally or, conversely, the impact of being a woman is the same for people with a disability as it is for people with no disability.

A third possibility, which we call non-additive disadvantage in Figure 1, is that while being a woman and having a disability are both associated with negative outcomes, the effect of disability is less for women than for men.[4] In the context of women and disability, non-additive disadvantage might be found if, for in-

---

[4] Berthoud uses the term 'logarithmic disadvantage' to refer to the same phenomenon.

stance, women with a disability were less limited than men with a disability, or if employers would prefer to employ men without a disability but do not differentiate among people with a disability on the basis of whether they are male or female.

The distinctions between the patterns of multiple disadvantage are important to understanding the processes involved and in terms of policy. For instance, a finding of exponential disadvantage would lead us to focus on the specific experiences of women with a disability, to use our present example, in order to understand their labour market participation. Additive disadvantage, on the other hand, would lead to positing two separate processes, one being gender-based and the other based on disability. Non-additive disadvantage, like exponential disadvantage, might lead us to focus on the specific experiences of men with a disability, in our example.

All of the examples above have assumed that women are at a higher risk of unfavourable outcomes. This is true of labour market participation, in general, but is not true of all outcomes. Men are disadvantaged in terms of life expectancy, for instance and, as we will see below, in terms of some of the outcomes studied in this paper, particularly low levels of educational achievement.

The measure of disability in the 2006 Census is based on the following question:

15. Do you have any of the following long-lasting conditions?

    a. Blindness, deafness or a severe vision or hearing impairment (yes, no)

    b. A condition that substantially limits one or more basic physical activities such as walking, climbing stairs, reaching, lifting or carrying (yes, no)

    c. A learning or intellectual disability (yes, no)

    d. A psychological or emotional condition (yes, no)

    e. Other, including any chronic illness (yes, no).

In this analysis, we distinguish between individuals with a physical disability (Yes to either a or b above) and individuals with a learning or intellectual disability (Yes to c above). Answers to these two questions suggested that just under 254,000 people in Ireland had a physical disability and that there were 70,870 people with a learning or intellectual disability. The distinction between physical disability and learning/intellectual disability is important in that the age profiles of the two types of disability are quite different, with learning/intellectual disability peaking in the teens (Watson and Nolan, 2010, forthcoming). The prevalence of other types of disability increases with age. Part of the reason for this is the lower life expectancy of many people with severe intellectual or learning disability (Patja et al., 2001) and part is also due to the fact that this kind of disability is likely to be particularly salient for young people who are at school, and is more likely to be noted at this stage. In the 25-44 age group, according to this measure, physical disability affects 2.4 per cent and learning/intellectual disability affects 1.2 per cent. Because of the large number of cases, the census data affords a unique opportunity to examine the situation of these groups.

The four outcomes we examine are:

- Low education: less than full second level education. Those still at school or college are excluded from this analysis. The net figures presented for differences by gender and disability status include controls for five-year age group, family status, religion, ethnicity, migration (whether ever lived outside Ireland and time since moved to Ireland) and location (urban/rural residence and region).

- Being outside the labour market: those still at school or college are excluded from this analysis and levels of education, as well as the other characteristics above, are controlled.

- Unemployed: The risk of unemployment for those in the labour market. Those outside the labour market are excluded in this analysis and education, as well as other characteristics, is controlled.

- Unskilled or semi-skilled manual social class: This is measured at the household level and is based on the usual occupation of the reference person in the household, who may be someone other than the adult concerned. For this analysis, education, as well as other characteristics, is controlled.

Education, labour market participation and social class can be seen as sequential events. Education is usually completed before the person enters the labour market and will affect the probability of entering the labour market, of finding work and the social class of the job obtained.

We might expect different patterns across these outcomes for a number of reasons. Education is typically completed relatively early in the person's life and will be strongly affected by family background as well as by the person's own abilities in school. When it comes to labour market participation, social perceptions of the appropriate adult roles for men and women (which have broadened for women but not for men in recent decades) come into play as well as the perceptions and preferences of employers. Social class is measured at the household level, so living arrangements as well as the person's own resources (mainly via their employment) will matter. To the extent that there are differences in living arrangements between women and men and between people with a disability and people without a disability, we might expect the patterns to be affected. As we focus on relatively young adults (aged 25-44) here, the age at which young people leave home and the rate at which they form partnerships will matter a great deal.

Low Levels of Education

Figure 2 shows the overall percentage of adults aged 25-44 with low levels of education by gender and disability. Those still at school or college are excluded from this analysis. Men in this age group are more likely than women to have left school before completing second level education (27 per cent compared to 20 per cent). People with a disability are much more likely to have low levels of education than non-disabled people: 45 per cent of people with a physical disability left school before completing second level education, while the figure for those with a learning/intellectual disability is 70 per cent. Note that we cannot be sure whether the disability was present when the person was still at school; it may have developed since that time.[5] As noted above, learning/intellectual disability is more likely than other types of disability to have been present from childhood, however, and its impact on education is very clear in Figure 2.

Figure 2 also shows the net (independent) effects of gender and disability when other relevant risk factors are controlled. These net figures control for five-year age group, nationality, ethnicity, religion, migration and location. They are based on a multivariate model and are presented for single white Irish Catholic adults with no children, age 25-29, living in Dublin and who have never lived outside Ireland. The differences by gender and by disability status remain when these other characteristics are controlled.

---

[5] Detailed results from the National Disability survey suggest that about half of people with a disability age 18-44 were affected by the disability before the age of 18, ranging from 21 per cent for pain disability to 86 per cent for intellectual or learning disability (CSO, 2008, Tables 14.2, 15.2, 16.2, 17.2, 18.2, 19.2, 20.2 and 21.2)

Figure 2: Gross and Net Risk of Low Education by Gender and by Disability for Adults Age 25-44

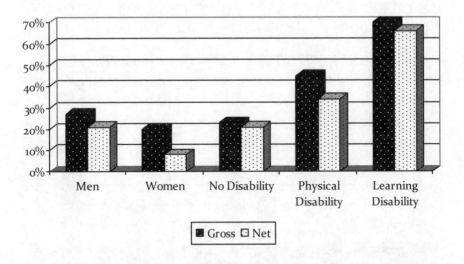

Source: Census 2006, special analysis. Net figures are those for white Irish Catholic single adults with no children, age 25-29, living in Dublin and who have never lived outside Ireland. For male/female net figures: person with no disability; for disability, net figures presented for men.

In the next figure, we examine the net impact of disability on education separately for men and women. As explained earlier, we show the expected risk of low education under two conditions: constraining the impact of disability to be the same for men and women (no interaction) and allowing the impact of disability to differ for men and women (interaction). Comparing the risks under the two conditions allows us to see whether the impact of disability on the risk of low education is different for men and women.

We can see from Figure 3 that when we take account of the gender-disability interaction, the expected percentage of men with low levels of education is very slightly lower in the case of physical disability (33 per cent vs. 34 per cent) and considerably lower in the case of learning disability (58 per cent vs. 66 per cent). On the other hand, the risk is slightly higher for women in the case of physical disability (16 vs. 15 per cent) and considerably higher for learning/intellectual disability (51 vs. 40 per cent). Having a learning disability, then, is associated with a smaller increase in educational disadvantage in men than in women.

Figure 3: Net Risk of Low Education by Gender and Disability under Two Conditions (with and without gender/disability interaction)

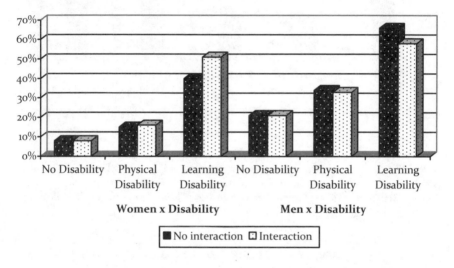

Source: Census 2006, special analysis. Figures are estimated for white Irish Catholic single adults with no children, age 25-29, living in Dublin and who have never lived outside Ireland.

These results – particularly for intellectual/learning disability – are an example of what we call non-additive disadvantage: both men and people with a disability are educationally disadvantaged, but men with a disability are less disadvantaged than we would expect if disability had the same impact on men and women. Note, however, that even though the pattern of disadvantage for men with a disability in the case of education is non-additive, the most disadvantaged group is men with a learning disability, 58 per cent of whom are expected to have low levels of education compared to 51 per cent of women with a learning disability.

The finding of a substantial gender interaction in the case of learning/intellectual disability would lead us to seek an explanation in the specific circumstances of women with this type of disability. This difference may be due the fact that the measure of learning/ intellectual disability used here is associated with a higher level of difficulty among women than among men (CSO, 2008, Table 3A).[6]

Outside the Labour Market

We turn now to our second outcome: being outside the labour market. Labour market participation is a key element in social inclusion (Berkel and Møller, 2002). Women's labour market participation is lower than that of men, as they remain most likely to take time off paid work to care for children (Treas and Drobnič, 2010) and other family members (Bolin, Lindgren and Lundborg, 2008). However, women who do combine work and family tend to have higher levels of life satisfaction (Kotowska et al., 2010) and improved mental health (Barnett, 2004).

Figure 4 shows that women aged 24-44 are about four times as likely as men in the same age group to be outside the labour market (24 per cent compared to 6 per cent). Note that students are excluded from these figures, so we are comparing people who are outside the labour market because they are engaged in home duties or unable to work due to illness or other reasons to those who are in the labour market and either at work or unemployed. This is the age group where women are most likely to have children and women are still the ones most likely to take time off paid work to care for children. The impact of disability is also very marked: people with either a physical or learning

---

[6] There is a difference between the census measure used here and National Disability Survey (NDS) measures of learning/intellectual disability in this regard. The NDS suggests that boys and girls with learning disability experience about the same level of difficulty with everyday activities (Watson and Nolan, 2010, Figure 12).

disability are 3.4-3.5 times as likely as those with no disability to be outside the labour market. Part of this difference will be due to the lower levels of educational attainment we saw above, but there are also likely to be additional barriers to labour market participation such as difficulties in physically gaining access to employment and prejudices of employers.

Figure 4: Gross and Net Risk of Being Outside the Labour Market by Gender and by Disability for Adults Age 25-44

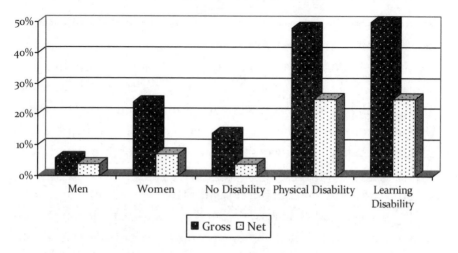

Source: Census 2006, special analysis. Net figures are those for white Irish Catholic single adults with no children, age 25-29, with lower second level education, living in Dublin and who have never lived outside Ireland. For men and women, net figures are for those with no disability; for disability status, net figures are for men.

The net figures control for education as well as five-year age group, nationality, ethnicity, religion, migration and location and are estimated for white Irish Catholic single adults with no children, with lower second level education, age 25-29, living in Dublin and who have never lived outside Ireland. The differences by gender are much smaller for this group because the labour force participation rate for single young women is much higher than that of married women. When we control for the association between disability and education, the gap in labour market participation between people with a disability and people without a disability is also very much reduced.

Figure 5 shows the impact of disability on the labour market participation of men and women, allowing the impact of disability to differ by gender. The figure shows that physical and learning/intellectual disability are associated with a reduction in labour force participation among both women and men, but that the impact of disability – especially physical disability – smaller for women. We see that the expected percentage outside the labour market falls for women but increases for men when we include the gender-disability interaction.

Figure 5: Net Risk of Being Outside the Labour Market by Gender and Disability under Two Conditions (with and without gender/disability interaction)

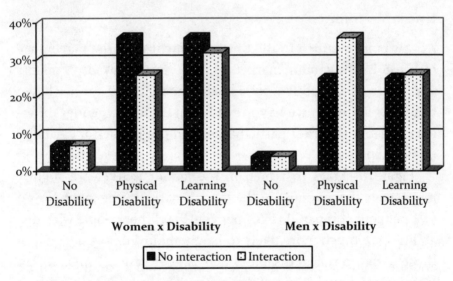

Source: Census 2006, special analysis. Figures are estimated for white Irish Catholic single adults with no children, age 25-29, with lower second level education, living in Dublin and who have never lived outside Ireland.

This is, again, an example of *non-additive disadvantage*: both women and people with a disability are less likely to participate in the labour market, but women with a disability are less disadvantaged than we would expect if disability had the same impact on women and men. This may arise because physical disabilities, in particular, cause more severe limitations in terms of men's participation in the lower-skilled manual occupations that are more common among men than women.

Another pattern that is evident when we allow the impact of disability to vary by gender is that intellectual/ learning disability has a greater impact than physical disability on the labour market participation of women while the reverse is true for men. This, again, may reflect differences in the requirements of occupations in which women and men with lower levels of education typically work and would direct our attention to the specific experiences of women with learning disabilities.

Unemployment

At this point we turn to the unemployment rate: the percentage of those in the labour market who are unemployed.[7] Students and other young adults outside the labour force are excluded from this figure, so we have already put aside the gender difference in labour marker participation and the impact of disability on participation.

Figure 6 shows that men in the labour market are slightly more likely than women in the labour market to be unemployed (7.4 per cent compared to 6.7 per cent) and that people with disabilities are much more likely to be unemployed: 16.5 per cent of those with a physical disability and 21.1 per cent of those with a learning disability. Some of this difference is undoubtedly due to the lower levels of education among people with disability. This can be seen when we focus on the net figures, which control for

---

[7] Note that this measure of unemployment is based on the person's self-reported main economic status, rather than the more stringent ILO definition used in the *Quarterly National Household Surveys*.

education as well as ethnicity, religion, nationality, migration and location and are presented for married white, Irish catholic adults with full second-level education. The gap between people with a disability and those with no disability is somewhat smaller – particularly in the case of learning disability.

Figure 6: Gross and Net Risk of Being Unemployed by Gender and by Disability for Adults Age 25-44

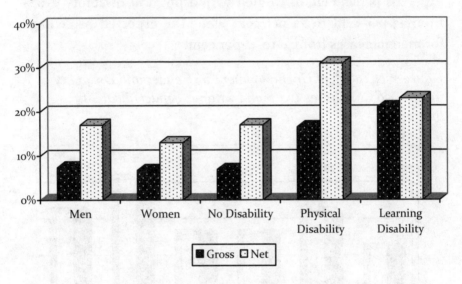

Source: Census 2006, special analysis. Net figures are those for white Irish Catholic single childless adults, age 25-29, with lower second level education, living in Dublin and who have never lived outside Ireland. For men and women, net figures are for those with no disability; for disability status, net figures are for men.

In Figure 7, we compare the net impact of having a disability on the unemployment rate for men and women before and after allowing the impact to differ by gender. We have controlled for five-year age group and level of education as well as other characteristics in order to highlight the net impact of unemployment. The difference based on disability is much less stark here than was in the case of labour market participation. This may arise if (as is very likely) people with a disability in the labour market tend to be less limited in their activities than people with a disability in general.

Nevertheless, people with disabilities are more likely to be unemployed. For both men and women, the impact of physical disability is larger than the impact of learning disability and the impact of physical disability is very slightly larger for men than for women. When we include the gender-interaction term, the expected percentage of women with a physical disability drops from 23 per cent to 22 per cent while the expected percentage for men increases from 31 to 32 per cent.

Figure 7: Net Risk of Unemployment by Gender and Disability under Two Conditions (with and without gender/disability interaction)

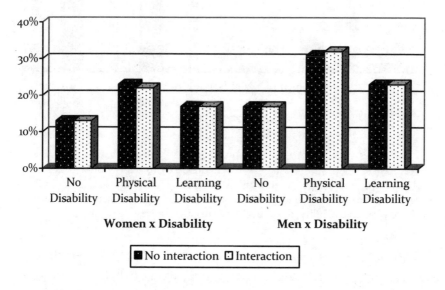

Source: Census 2006, special analysis. Figures are estimated for white Irish Catholic single adults with no children, age 25-29, with lower second level education, living in Dublin and who have never lived outside Ireland.

The pattern for men and physical disability is an example of *exponential disadvantage* with respect to unemployment, albeit a relatively weak one: men and people with physical disability are both more likely to be unemployed and men with a physical disability are even more likely to be unemployed than we would expect from the combination of the two effects (being male and having a physical disability).

The impact of learning disability is very similar for men and women: the expected percentage unemployed is the same when we include the interaction, as when we constrain the impact of having a disability to be the same for men and women. The pattern for men and learning disability, then, is an example of *additive disadvantage*: having a disability increases the risk of unemployment by about the same amount for men and women.

Lower Manual Social Class

The lower manual (unskilled and semi-skilled manual) social classes have been shown elsewhere to be at greater risk of poverty and deprivation than the skilled manual social class or the non-manual social classes (e.g. Whelan et al., 2001, 2003, 2004; Watson et al., 2009; Vandecasteele, 2010). Social class is measured at the household level, based on the occupation of the reference person. This means that men and women living in the same household will be assigned to the same social class, so that any differences between men and women overall will be driven by differences in class position between men and women living in different households. Similarly, to the extent that young adults with disability are still living with their (presumably non-disabled) families, their social class position will be derived from that of the reference person in the household. Figure 8 shows the gross and net risk of being in these social classes by gender and by disability.

We can see from Figure 8 that men, overall, are more likely than women to be in the lower manual social class (21 per cent compared to 16 per cent). This is partly due to the fact that young men are at higher risk of having lower levels of education, as we saw earlier. However, the gender difference remains when we control for education and other characteristics, as seen in the net figures in Figure 8.

Younger single adults with lower-second level education (the reference category for the net figures) are more likely than adults in the 25-44 age group as a whole to be in the lower manual social class, so that the net percentages are higher than the gross figures. There is still a gap between people with disability and those with no disability: 35 per cent of young adults with physical disability and 36 per cent of young adults with learning or intellectual disability are in the lower manual social class compared to 32 per cent of adults without a disability.

Figure 8: Gross and Net Risk of Being in the Unskilled or Semi-skilled Manual Social Class by Gender and by Disability for Adults Age 25-44

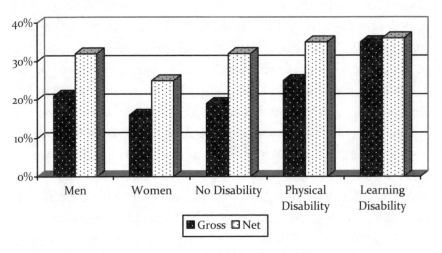

Source: Census 2006, special analysis. Net figures are those for white Irish Catholic single adults with no children, age 25-39, with lower second level education, living in Dublin and who have never lived outside Ireland. For men and women, net figures are for those with no disability; for disability status, net figures are for men.

In Figure 9, we compare the net impact of having a disability on the probability of being in the lower manual social class for men and women before and after allowing the impact to differ by gender. In general, the group differences are small because much of the difference has been captured by levels of education, which are controlled. For both men and women, those with a physical disability are more likely to be in the lower manual social class, but the difference is small and is equal under the two conditions (with the interaction and without the interaction). This suggests that much of the disadvantage experienced by people with physical disability that we saw in Figure 8 is driven by their lower levels of education. The similarity in the impact of disability on the social class position of women and men means that this is another example of *additive disadvantage*: men and people with a disability are at higher risk of being in the lower manual social classes and the risk for men with a disability is no greater than we would expect from the sum of these two risks.

Figure 9: Net Risk of Being in Lower Manual Social Class by Gender and Disability under Two Conditions (with and without gender/disability interaction)

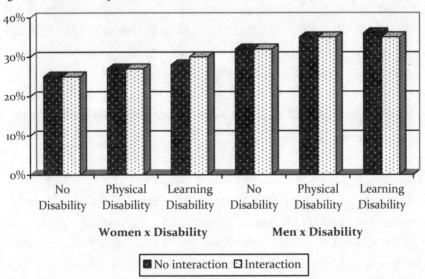

Source: Census 2006, special analysis. Figures are estimated for white Irish Catholic single adults with no children, age 25-29, with lower second level education, living in Dublin and who have never lived outside Ireland.

The pattern for learning disability is different for men and women. Although the difference is not large, the risk is slightly larger for women. When we allow the impact of intellectual/learning disability to differ by gender, the expected percentage of women in the unskilled or semi-skilled manual social class increases slightly (from 28 to 30 per cent) while the percentage for men falls slightly (from 36 to 35 per cent).

This can be seen as an example of *non-additive disadvantage* for men and learning disability with respect to social class: membership in each group is associated with a higher risk but membership in both groups is associated with a smaller risk than we would expect if the impact of having a learning disability were the same for men as it is for women.

Conclusion

In this paper, we drew on the typologies advanced by Berthoud to ask in what sense the risks of negative outcomes are 'worse' for members of two disadvantaged groups. We took groups based on gender and disability status and examined four outcomes using data from the 2006 census: low levels of education, non-participation in the labour market, unemployment and membership of the unskilled or semi-skilled manual social class. After presenting the overall differences by gender and disability status, we examined the net group differences based on joint group membership with other factors controlled (family status, religion, ethnicity, nationality, migration and location). The results for net differences in non-participation in the labour market, unemployment and social class also controlled for education.

For each of the four outcomes, we presented results for two interactions: being female (or male for outcomes where men are disadvantaged relative to women) and having a physical disability and being female (or male) and having a learning disability.

This gives a total of eight interactions and their location in relation to Berthoud's categories is shown in Figure 10.

In general, for the groups and outcomes examined, the most common pattern was that of non-additive disadvantage, or what Berthoud calls logarithmic disadvantage. In this pattern, each of two groups is at increased risk of a negative outcome relative to non-members, but membership in both groups is associated with a lower risk than we would expect from adding the two risks together. This pattern was found for five of the eight interactions examined.

Figure 10: Examples of Different Kinds of Multiple Disadvantage for Gender and Disability

Outcome	Groups	Type of Multiple Disadvantage
Low education	Male, physical disability	Non-additive
	Male, learning disability	Non-additive
Non-participation in labour market	Female, physical disability	Non-additive
	Female, learning disability	Non-additive
Unemployment	Male, physical disability	Exponential (weak)
	Male, learning disability	Additive
Unskilled/semi-skilled manual social class	Male, physical disability	Additive (weak)
	Male, learning disability	Non-additive

The concept of redundancy is useful in understanding why a non-additive pattern may arise. Redundancy can occur when the relationship between two predictors is very strong. Here, for instance, we found a very strong association between learning or intellectual disability and low levels of education. As a result, we cannot explain much of the additional variation in labour market outcomes by adding learning/intellectual disability to a model which already includes education. The combined effect is one of redundancy rather than accumulation (Nolan and Whelan, 1999, pp. 10-11).

There were two examples of additive disadvantage, but one of these was a weak pattern where the group differences were very small. Additive disadvantage describes the pattern where members of each group are disadvantaged relative to non-members, and membership in both groups is associated with a level of disadvantage approximately equal to what we would expect from the combination of membership in each. In this sense, membership in both groups is 'worse' than membership in either one, but not enough worse to prompt us to examine the unique circumstances of joint group membership in order to seek an explanation.

There was only one weak example of exponential disadvantage: membership of each group is associated with negative outcomes and members of both groups are even more disadvantaged than we would expect from combining the effects of membership in each one. This example was found for being male and physical disability for the outcome unemployment. The impact of physical disability on unemployment risk was slightly greater for men than for women, with other characteristics controlled. This is likely to be because of the greater importance of physical strength to many of the traditionally male-dominated manual occupations, so that physical disability may be a greater barrier to men than to women in finding suitable work.

The second general finding of note is that the pattern of multiple disadvantage can vary depending on the outcome we are examining. For instance, being male and having a physical disability fits the pattern of non-additive disadvantage for low education, weakly fits the pattern of exponential disadvantage for unemployment and additive disadvantage for lower manual social class.

A third point worth noting is that the absence of a pattern of exponential or additive disadvantage does not necessarily mean that a group is not 'worse off' in the sense of having a high risk of a negative outcome. For instance, we found a strong pattern of non-additive disadvantage in the case of men and learning disability for educational outcomes: the increased risk of low education associated with being a man with a disability was less than we would expect from the risks associated with each separately. However, it was still the case that men with a learning disability had the highest risk of being educationally disadvantaged. This is because the risk of this outcome is much higher for men than for women.

Fourthly, we were able to examine whether the increased risk of negative outcomes for people with a disability was cumulative, in the sense of finding an additional risk for labour market outcomes when education is controlled. People with a disability, particularly those with a learning disability, are at a strong disadvantage in terms of education. However, even with education controlled, people with a disability experience an additional risk of being outside the labour market, of unemployment and of being in a lower social class. Although we cannot be sure of the direction of causation with cross-sectional data, this suggests that the disadvantages associated with disability may cumulate across life-cycle stages

Finally, when a significant interaction indicates non-additive or exponential disadvantage, it directs our attention to the specific circumstances of one group. The finding of exponential disadvantage in the case of unemployment for men with a physical disability leads us to seek an explanation in some specific aspects of the physical disability of men or the impact it has on their employment prospects. Similarly, we found non-additive disadvantage in the case of being male and learning disability for the outcome low education. In this case, it was the gender not initially at higher risk that experienced the biggest increase in risk of the negative outcome as a result of learning disability. This finding draws our attention to the specific situation of women with a learning disability in order to understand its impact on education and lead us to hypothesise that – at least based on the measure of learning/intellectual disability in the Census – women with this type of disability experience a greater level of limitation.

In general, the analyses in this paper point to the importance of paying careful attention to the processes underlying disadvantage and the ways in which these may interact. It cannot be assumed that where membership in each of two groups is associated with a negative outcome, members of both groups will be 'doubly disadvantaged', or indeed that a pattern found for one outcome will be found for others. We saw in the case of labour market participation, for instance, that the barriers to participation may be quite different for men and women and that characteristics of many traditionally male jobs may result in particular barriers for men with a physical disability. Exploring the patterns of multiple disadvantage is useful in drawing attention to areas where the interaction of different processes – education, labour market and lifecycle processes – may result in unexpected outcomes.

References

Barrett, A. and McCarthy, Y. (2007) 'The Earnings of Immigrants In Ireland: Results From the 2005 EU Survey Of Income And Living Conditions'. In *Quarterly Economic Commentary, Winter*. Dublin: Economic and Social Research Institute.

Barnett, R.C. (2004) 'Women and Multiple Roles: Myths and Reality'. *Harvard Review of Psychiatry* 12(3), 158-164.

Berkel, R. van and Møller, I.H. (eds.) (2002) *Active social policies in the EU: Inclusion through participation?* Bristol: The Policy Press.

Berthoud, R. (1976) *The Disadvantages of Inequality*. London: Macdonald & Jane's.

Berthoud, R. (2003) *Multiple disadvantage in Employment: A quantitative analysis*. York: Joseph Rowntree Foundation.

Bevelander, P. and Groeneveld, S. (2007) 'How Many Hours Do You Have to Work to Be Integrated? Full Time and Part Time Employment of Native and Ethnic Minority Women in the Netherlands' IZA Discussion Paper No. 2684. Available at SSRN: http://ssrn.com/abstract=978783.

Bolin, K., Lindgren, B. and Lundborg, P. (2008). 'Your next of kin or your own career?: Caring and working among the 50+ of Europe,' *Journal of Health Economics*, Elsevier, Vol. 27(3), pp. 718-738, May.

Central Statistics Office (2008), *National Disability Survey 2006, First Report*, Dublin: Stationery Office.

Duncan, O.D. (1968) 'Inheritance of poverty or inheritance of race?' In: D.P. Moynihan (ed.), *On Understanding Poverty*, New York: Basic Books, pp. 85–110.

Layte, R. and Whelan, C.T. (2002) 'Cumulative Disadvantage or Individualisation? A comparative analysis of poverty risk and incidence'. *European Societies* 4(2) 2002: 209–233.

Kotowska, I.E., Matysiak, A., and Stryc, M. (2010). *Family Life and Work: Second European Quality of Life Survey*. Dublin: European Foundation for the Improvement of Living and Working Conditions.

Nolan, B. and Whelan, C.T. (1999) *Loading the Dice? A Study of Cumulative Disadvantage*. Dublin: Oak Tree Press in association with the Combat Poverty Agency.

Patja, K., Iivanainen, M., Vesala, H., Oksanen, H. and Ruoppila, I. (2001) 'Life expectancy of people with intellectual disability: A 35-year follow-up study.' *Journal of Intellectual Disability Research*, Vol. 44, Issue 5, pp. 591–599.

Treas, J. and Drobnič, S. (eds) (2010) *Dividing the Domestic: Men, Women, and Household Work in Cross-National Perspective*. Studies in Inequality Series. Stanford, CA: Stanford University Press.

Vandecasteele, L. (2010). 'Life Course Risks or Cumulative Disadvantage? The Structuring Effect of Social Stratification Determinants and Life

Course Events on Poverty Transitions in Europe.' *European Sociological Review*, Advance Access published 11 March.

Watson, D., Whelan C.T and Maître, B. (2009) 'Class and Poverty: Cross-sectional and dynamic analysis of income poverty and life-style deprivation' in Rose, D. and Harrison, E (eds.) *Social Class in Europe: An Introduction to the European Socio-Economic Classification*. London: Routledge.

Watson, D., Lunn P., Quinn E. and Russell, H. (forthcoming) *Multiple Inequalities in Ireland: An Analysis of Census 2006* Dublin: The Equality Authority and The Economic and Social Research Institute

Watson, D. and Nolan, B. (2010) *A Social Portrait of People with Disability in Ireland*. Dublin: The Department of Community, Equality and Gaeltacht Affairs.

Whelan, C.T., Layte, R., Maitre, B. and Nolan, B. (2001), 'Income, Deprivation and Economic Strain: An Analysis of the European Community Household Panel', *European Sociological Review*, 17, 4: 357-372.

Whelan, C.T., Layte, R. and Maître B. (2003), 'Persistent Income Poverty and Deprivation in the European Union', *Journal of Social Policy*, 3, 1:1-18.